Testimonials

"Performance in any field is much more than running faster and becoming stronger. Performance is also between the ears. Scott Fox, Dr. Bob, and the team at Vital 100 Wellness truly understand how to get our team to perform at a much higher level and I am certain they will do the same for your business. When Dr. Bob, Scott Fox and his team talk, I urge you to listen. They know their stuff. All issues in my life seem much easier to achieve with the clarity and approach they provided."

D. Farris

"My life was a mess until I began working with Dr. Bob and his team. I was always exhausted, could not sleep and could not handle any stress. Within two months of working with Dr. Bob my life and my family's lives are in a different place and we can function at a much higher level."

L. Styles

"If ever you get a chance to work with Vital 100 Wellness don't even give it a second thought. Dr. Bob is the most knowledgeable and compassionate person in health I have ever met. He will change your life and those around you for the better."

T. Faroque

"Vital 100 Wellness helped me get to an amazingly healthy place in my life, and I am very thankful for that. The best part though, is that I now understand how to stay healthy. Dr. Bob has a very comforting way of explaining everything he taught my staff and me. By the way, the quarter following our work with him was our best quarter by far. As a direct result of working with him our bottom line increased by more than 7 percent."

B. Sampson

"Many doctors tried to get me healthy, so I could enjoy my life. I had little success until meeting Dr. Bob. Although he had different ways of looking at my health, he changed my life big-time. Everyone who wants a healthy and productive life should contact Dr. Bob and his team. Specifically, my memory and energy levels have improved dramatically since working with his team."

G. Artesmore

SKYROCKET YOUR BOTTOM LINE

Escalate Your Business
and Personal Bottom Line
With a Proven Blueprint

ROBERT JOHNSON

Skyrocket Your Bottom Line

The Program That Will Raise Any Company's Bottom Line To The Top

ISBN: (hardcover)

ISBN: 979-8-88759-753-9 - paperback

ISBN: 979-8-88759-754-6 - ebook

Cover design by Jude Mag-asin

Printed in the USA.

Thank you for purchasing *Skyrocket Your Bottom Line!* I'm excited to share my knowledge to help you with your bottom line. As a bonus for buying this book, I'm offering a Free Health Assessment to help you get started right away. Just head on over to my website (www.vital100wellness.com) to claim yours today!

Additionally, if you'd like more information or to discuss your thoughts on this book or some specifics that might further help you personally, then I encourage you to copy the link below into your browser so we can connect. You can also stay updated on additional tips and tools if you subscribe.
I'm excited about your progress!

Here's to your health and success,
~Dr. Bob Johnson
www.vital100wellness.com

Skyrocketing Your Bottom Line is dedicated to my parents, Sam and Bette Johnson, who continually encouraged me and offered role models that allowed me to develop life values that helped encourage me to become positive, passionate, caring for those around me and to be eternally motivated in everything I do.

I also dedicate Skyrocketing Your Bottom Line to my two sons, Andrew and Nicolas Johnson, who have provided me with the qualities of purpose, humility and unconditional love.

Preface

Supercharge Your Bottom Line

Should you be concerned about your bottom line? Business owners, CEOs, presidents, performance coaches, and administrators are urged to take notice if:

- Your services and product lines are excellent and your marketing is robust, yet your bottom line is anemic.
- You spend far too much time, resources, and energy resolving disputes and damaging communication within your organization and to potential or existing clients.
- Your workforce is always shorthanded and rarely focused.
- Too many within your workforce are leaving and disrupting functionality.
- You dread beginning the day because your days rarely run smoothly.

If you experience any of the above or, worse, several of these situations, your corporate culture and bottom line require a shot in the arm, if not restructuring.

Skyrocket Your Bottom Line will show you how successful companies, organizations, and teams utilize innovative wellness enhancement, communication skill development, and evolution of the collective performance mindset to supercharge their overall performance and, ultimately, their bottom line.

Why You Should Read This Book

Any CEO or top executive has the goal and dream of driving their company or organization's bottom line to a higher, more profitable level in order to live a better quality of life.

You may feel you have the services or products that potential customers or clients want, and you have many of the pieces in place to make your business undertaking a robust success. In fact, you have been profitable (or at least paying the bills and covering overhead) in the past or at present, yet you cannot reach your optimal goals or become highly profitable.

Worse yet, your cash flow does not cover your overhead, and you are operating in the RED.

You may have already made strides toward success:

- You have tried many types of marketing and offered bonuses to top producers.

- You have altered your products, services and distribution channels with minimal changes.
- You have even hired consultants who produced temporary successes which could not be sustained.

However, with your lack of success, you go home every evening wondering and anxious about what you can do to help your organization be more successful or, in your wildest dreams, *highly* successful and, of course, highly profitable.

If any part of this resembles your company or organization, answers and solutions do exist to drive your company to levels not previously imagined. In fact, despite a plethora of studies and myriad anecdotes touting positive results, few companies know how the program described in this book can profoundly impact your bottom line.

The program covered in this book involves the physical, mental, and emotional health of your entire organization and how every person acquires the knowledge and skills to communicate to every member within your company or organization and to existing and potential customers and clients outside your company.

I can read your mind: "How can the health and communication skills of every member of our organization profoundly and positively affect our bottom line?" I want you to briefly suspend your disbelief that this program could make such a difference to your company to skyrocket your bottom line to levels you had not even imagined. Furthermore, I would understand if you are silently thinking, "My people are healthy, and they communicate very well, thank you."

I would respectfully disagree with that thought as I have worked with many clients and patients who thought they were healthy, yet upon utilizing our unique assessment tools, interviews and surveys, we helped them discover several physical, mental, and emotional issues that, when corrected, positively altered their lives and their production significantly.

Likewise, when taught and trained in the latest communication skills refined through highly validated studies, top salespeople and executives who were otherwise very successful raised their success bars individually and collectively.

One of the peripheral bonuses with these components I will describe in detail (conceptually and practically) within this book is that everyone will take their newly found health, higher energy, improved focus and enhanced communication skills to incorporate them into every facet and relationship in their lives. This is the foundation for a vastly improved quality of life, both in their professional and personal lives.

By utilizing the different components of this program within your company or organization, you will not only raise your bottom line to levels you could not have previously envisioned but (and this is big) you and your executives, decision-makers and implementers will be viewed very positively as caring, compassionate and very intuitive.

This corporate wellness program will take your company, organization or team to extraordinary levels and employees, customers, clients and families inside and outside will view your company positively on many levels. This is the basis for a highly successful company that results in improved sales and creates a happier work and sales force, which has also demonstrated through many studies to improve retention and recruitment. This book will help you implement and customize a corporate wellness program and develop communication skills second to none. These skills developed in your workforce will send your bottom line to new heights where it is healthier, happier, and more productive. You (CEO, owner, executive, director) will also be much happier, more productive personally, and much less stressed.

I also want you to realize that if you decide to work with our team, you are working with people who "walk their talk." We personally practice and thoroughly embody health and relationship-building communication skills.

If you want to contact us to either find out more about how we can take your bottom line to new heights or you actually want to engage our services, contact me directly at: drbob@vital100wellness.com.

Author's Note

Why I wrote This Book

Organizations (companies, teams, groups) all struggle for survival, whether it's their financials, market competition or corporate culture. What most organizations and companies can control is what they focus on. This includes their products, product development, management and marketing. Although these are indispensable and critical areas for a company, there are equally important areas a company should focus on, which are often ignored yet will undermine a company's success.

These areas include:

- The health, energy, and focus of each member within a group, including executives and employees.
- Communication skills within an organization as well as with potential customers or clients.
- The performance mindset, so critical to optimal performance.

- The overall corporate culture (i.e., the totality of interactions), civility, and the smoothness of operations.

When optimized, these areas will make the difference between a struggling or failed company and a highly successful, profitable company. I wrote this book to make the difference for a CEO, owner, leader or aspiring business developer to grasp those areas that will optimize their company or business.

This book will not only help a company leader realize how critical these "softer" areas are, but help develop programs to implement strategies to optimize their business or organization. A comprehensive corporate performance enhancement program assists companies in developing customized programs that will help their organization exceed its most optimistic goals.

What You Will Learn

Optimizing your performance (individually or collectively) and bottom line are truly learned skills calling into play many areas of a business organization's operation and function. The first is to learn what skills and strengths a company possesses and which areas will need the assistance of experts. Vital 100 Wellness is a program that brings critical areas of expertise necessary to take a company or organization to high levels of performance and profitability.

Does your company or organization (new or long-term) know how to optimize the health, energy, dedication and focus of its executives or workforce? Does your company utilize the communication skills that will optimize performance, or does it possess an optimal performance mindset? These are all critical questions that need answers if your company wants to enhance and skyrocket your bottom line.

A skilled program will enhance these areas within a company, team or organization. Most importantly, a CEO, owner or leader will become aware of these areas' importance in building an extraordinary business with optimized performance and an exceptional bottom line.

What This Book Will Do for You

I share the blueprint for CEOs, owners and leaders in companies and organizations of all sizes and in all niches for optimizing areas in which they are not qualified or have expertise. These areas are critical for the success of your company, organization or group.

You will need to manage the quality of health, vitality and communication skills (within your company or to outside clients) and promote the performance mindset of every person in your organization. This includes all leaders and members of your workforce. This book will provide the blueprint and understanding of why these areas are critical and how to find the answers to optimize critical areas all businesses and organizations will need to manage, whether they realize how critical they are.

Developing a superior corporate culture and the quality of every organization member (health, energy, communication and performance mindset) will bring a company or organization to the top of its "food chain."

This program will be your passport to achieving bottom line and performance goals and establishing a corporate culture in which every member will want to become a truly integral component as opposed to an interchangeable piece. They will want to invest their passion, energy and precious time.

Our goal for you is to be a partner with your company, organization or group in your journey to achieve greatness. Contact drbob@vital100wellness.com to understand how this comprehensive, customized program can optimize your company or organization's performance.

Table of Contents

Introduction

Our Bottom Line Enhancement Program

I have found that through several careers, businesses, projects and competition in high-level athletics, the program or undertaking, no matter how effective, is only as good as the passion and communication skills of the person and group overseeing or administering that program.

I always feel that the company or organization we work with is fortunate to work with such a passionate organization that embodies everything we teach others.

In 1981, the director of my hospital residency (I was one of four residents), upon hearing I had won the Montreal International Marathon the weekend before, said that "the hospital residency was not giving me enough work" because I was able to win an international marathon. Being a resident in a highly demanding, time-consuming hospital program exhausted my fellow residents, yet it was my passion, positivity and energy that allowed me to function at a high level in several demanding roles, which also included being a newlywed two months before my marathon success.

As the founding member and co-owner of a corporate wellness program, I have brought together equally passionate people to help raise the bottom lines and performance of organizations and companies. As a result, not only will your company or organization be the recipient of an amazing, highly researched and effective program and information, but your organization or business will be exposed to a passion and energy that is truly contagious.

Effective programs delivered with passion and high energy combined with the willingness of an organization or company to entertain change is the formula to raise the bottom line of companies and organizations from newly launched to high-flying companies.

If every member (or at least a majority of members) of an organization or company can raise their collective energy, focus, overall health and communication skills by a minimum of 10 percent (our experience delivers much greater than 10 percent), their overall performance will exceed all expectations. The goal of our company is to raise your performance by significantly greater than 10 percent. This book will detail the aspects of our corporate wellness and bottom-line enhancing program and how it will directly and positively affect your company, organization, team and all the individuals involved.

I also describe how each part of this program is incorporated and maintained over time within your company or organization until your bottom line and corporate culture goals are realized or exceeded. If you value your company and feel you have not reached your potential, I strongly encourage you to study this book. And if you want to further your success, contact me directly at

drbob@vital100wellness.com to see how we can customize our corporate wellness, communication and bottom-line enhancement program to your unique organizational or corporate needs.

Upgrading health, focus, energy and communication skills will improve the performance of individuals and groups. The concepts are simple. The implementation is a bit more difficult, but the results are amazing and worth the time and effort. Each organization is unique in its particular needs and willingness to embrace change to achieve a higher and more robust level of performance. As a result, the time it will take to reach a company's or organization's goals will vary. During our time with a company or organization, we can better clarify the time necessary to achieve the initial desired goals.

Reaching an organization's goals and installing programs to maintain the results will require flexibility in the time necessary to achieve the desired result.

The next chapter discusses the key components of *Skyrocketing Your Bottom Line*. However, knowing your goals is essential to the process, so I highly recommend you think about what that success looks like to you. Write down at least three goals you would like to accomplish in the near future, then let's get started.

Chapter 1

The Key Components of Your Bottom Line

Owners and leaders of companies and organizations are focused on driving their companies through product development, innovation, and greater sales while lowering the cost of doing business. These are indeed critical components of a profitable and sustainable business. Without the proper components in place, a company or organization will probably fail. These critical components are influenced by:

- Poor products or services.
- Poor sales strategies.
- Ineffective promotions delivered by ineffective salespeople.
- High production costs.

While these are important, few CEOs and leaders realize the importance of soft, less measurable, yet more hidden components that will ramp up their bottom line. These are the components that most owners and CEOs don't realize can dramatically skyrocket their business or undermine a company or organization if ignored. These less obvious components greatly contribute to the success of a company, organization or team and make that group a more enjoyable, productive environment. These components are:

- The health, focus and enthusiasm levels of every individual in an organization or company.
- The ability of every individual to communicate effectively within the company and with potential clients, customers and other groups.

Companies with Mediocre Products Can Still Produce Profitable Results

Many studies have shown that the wellness, enthusiasm and communication levels of executives and the workforce can improve the bottom line by as much as 30 to 50 percent.[1] Microsoft is an example of a highly successful company that had mediocre products but parlayed a fantastic corporate culture, exceptional communication skills and effective, groundbreaking marketing with a highly enthusiastic workforce to become outrageously profitable. Microsoft is an excellent example of how to run a business, even if they are promoting average products and services.

Microsoft demonstrated the importance of the soft and less appreciated skills to become a model company. There

1 Dr. Steve Aldana, "The 7 Best Reasons to Have a Wellness Program in 2023," Employee Wellness Programs, February 16, 2023, https://www.wellsteps.com/blog/2020/01/02/reasons-to-have-a-wellness-program-benefits-of-wellness/.

have also been many examples of teams in all different sports that used exceptional communication skills and enthusiastic, high-energy, motivated players with few recognized superstars to achieve their ultimate championship goals. The classic example of that was the 1969 New York Mets, who won the Major League World Series and will be remembered in sports lore as the *Amazin' Mets*, a team composed of average players, save two or three superstars.

What a company, team or organization invests in their workforce in health, performance and communication always yields amazing results. If a company or team is lucky enough to have great products with a stellar business plan combined with the skills mentioned above and an enthusiasm promoting culture, the bottom line will go through the roof.

Whether a company, team or organization has stellar products and superstar members or they are promoting mediocre products and services with average personnel, by developing an exceptional culture, coaching the workforce or its members about how to be optimally healthy while utilizing excellent communication skills within a focused, high energy environment there will be a positive impact on your bottom line. In addition, a highly desirable culture combined with a winning, highly profitable bottom line will also have beneficial ripple effects throughout the organization and into the community outside the organization.

The message here is that an investment in a wellness program that develops the skills, enthusiasm, and winning mindset focus within an organization will yield significant, positive results within an evolving, desirable working environment that will appeal to the customers and applicants the organization is ultimately seeking to attract. The health (body and brain) of every person in a company will allow them to function at a much higher level, and they will rarely be absent.

Success and Your Brain: Understanding Brain Function and Its Optimization

The most important tool necessary to control health and to optimize performance is your brain. The brain oversees how all the tissues, organs and systems of the body function.

If your brain (more appropriately the central nervous system) is degenerating, you will not be able to think, strategize and perform basic coordinated movements, balance the entire hormonal system, stave off major infections and just perform basic functions. With a poor or degenerating brain, we are more like reptiles with little more than reactionary survival skills.

When we are born, we have all the brain cells (neurons) we will ever have. Throughout our lives we continue to lose or kill brain cells due to toxins (e.g. mercury, pesticides, mold toxins), infections (herpes, covid viruses, Epstein-Barr, viruses, etc), inflammation due to concussions or trauma or an inadequate supply of nutrients or oxygen. Although it is critical to mitigate loss of nerve cells throughout our lives, a more important strategy for optimizing brain function is to continually improve the connectivity, efficiency and communication between nerve cells. This is done via continual mental stimulation, proper amounts of nutrients such as essential fatty acids, glucose (the "food" for brain function and energy production) and, of course, oxygen.

Extrapolating this to performance (athletic, mental and even emotional) optimizing brain function is critical for improving performance while a degenerating, non-evolving or traumatized brain will eventually equate to decreasing performance and a poorer bottom line.

It is important to understand that different parts of the brain perform different functions and that the degeneration of one part of the brain does not necessarily condemn other parts of the brain.

An example of isolated brain degeneration happens when a stroke (blood vessel rupture or closure) compromises or paralyzes a specific area of the body but doesn't affect cognitive abilities or the ability to breathe.

Nevertheless, compromising issues (trauma, poor nutrients, etc.) will eventually negatively impact all of your brain's neurons and the entire brain. This may lead to overall brain degeneration, such as dementia.

The areas of the brain and what functions they serve are important to understand. Most parts of the brain have a right and left division of labor in which the right brain controls the left side of the body and the left brain controls the right side of the body.

Temporal Lobe

This lobe is on the sides of the brain and is involved with hearing, language, verbal memory, recall of learned facts, unemotional speech, music interaction, long-term memory and energy levels throughout the day.

Occipital Lobe

This lobe is located on the top back of the brain and is involved with written text, colors and coordination of hand-eye movements.

Frontal Cortex

This part of the brain is located behind the forehead and the top front of the brain and is involved with detailed hand coordination, decisions, social behavior, decisions about desires, motivations, attention and concentration.

Parietal Lobe

This part of the brain is located on top and side of the brain and is involved with sensitivities to touch or pain, special awareness, right left discrimination, handwriting, math, word and symbol selection and recognition.

Brain Stem

This part of the brain is located at the bottom of the brain leading to the spinal cord and is involved with swallowing, bowel movement and motility, bloating after meals, dry eyes and dry mouth, racing or fluttering of the heart, bowel and bladder control.

Basal Ganglia (Indirect and Direct)

This part of the brain is located in the middle of the brain and is involved in speed of movement, muscle stiffness, stooped posture, hand cramping, abnormal body movements, constantly nervous, restless mind, compulsive behavior and increased tightness and tone of the most muscles.

Cerebellum

This part of the brain is located at the lower back of the brain and is involved in balance, dizziness, nausea or car sickness, immediate impact when drinking alcohol, back muscles and chronic neck or back tightness.

A questionnaire (Brain Function Assessment Form) can easily help identify which area of the brain is being affected with degeneration or trauma and guide early identification and targeted treatment or rehabilitation.

There is a direct correlation between brain function and performance. If a particular area of the brain is degenerating and that area controls a critical function involved in performance, then the bottom line will be negatively impacted.

On the other hand, if your performance (and the bottom line) is contingent on how well that connected area is functioning, it would make sense to improve performance by directing strategies to optimize that part of the brain, not to mention the improvement of overall brain function.

The performance of individuals, organizations, companies and teams is contingent on the collective health, capability and function of every individual involved, especially each brain.

These factors are all initially critical for optimal brain function for individuals and, ultimately, for an organization.

- The health of the corporate culture.
- Mental, physical and emotional stimulation.
- Optimal brain nutrition.
- Appropriate sleep for daily recovery and brain cleansing.
- Balance between pushing to meet goals and deadlines and a stress-managed environment.
- A healthy environment in which to work.
- Appropriate and effective communication.
- Job descriptions that optimize each person's strengths and overall performance.

- A wellness program that helps each executive and workforce member to stop brain degeneration while upgrading brain performance.

A program disseminating information that improves performance, motivation, communication and health while continuing to upgrade every person's bottom line is an investment that will multiply returns many-fold.

An ideal corporate wellness program should include the brain wellness questionnaire (Brain Function Assessment Form) for every individual contributing to an organization's bottom line, followed by interpretation with an action plan to optimize each person's bottom line.

Genetics: A Critical Guide to Health and Performance

The genetic code we are all given at conception by our biologic mother and father is unique for every individual except for identical siblings. Our genetics dictate much of our overall health and susceptibility to contracting illness.

The term "genotype" is the combination of the genetic code our parents give us. Yet, the expression of our genes is called our phenotype: the interaction of our genes with our lifestyle and environment.

An example of the phenotype health expression is when our genetics make us susceptible to heart disease (e.g., if our father or mother had heart disease). Yet knowing our genetic destiny, we can eat healthily, exercise regularly and conduct our lives to counteract that genetic susceptibility to heart disease to increase our chances of never having or reducing the effects.

The key with our genotype and phenotype is to identify what genetic weaknesses and strengths we have and what actions and lifestyle to pursue to strengthen our genetic weaknesses and support our strengths.

Genetic testing has evolved in the last 20 years to simply and cost-effectively be able to determine our genotype. Once your genotype is known, lifestyle strategies can be planned or actually suggested by the genetic test. This will serve as a blueprint for becoming optimally healthy and productive.

The test now utilized by Genetic Direction will guide and help optimize:

- Weight loss strategies.
- Immune enhancement for disease resistance.
- Nutritional intake.
- Types, frequency and intensity of exercise.
- Detoxification ability.
- Sleep for optimal health.
- Addiction potential.
- Hormone optimization and more.

In a setting (corporation, organization, team), it is critical to determine how to optimize every member's performance via their present health condition and how they will respond to lifestyle choices to maximize their short-term and long-term performance.

Simple genetic testing is a critical health assessment tool. When combined with other precise tools and technology, it will eliminate guesswork to optimize your executives' and workforce's outcomes and your company, organization and team's bottom line.

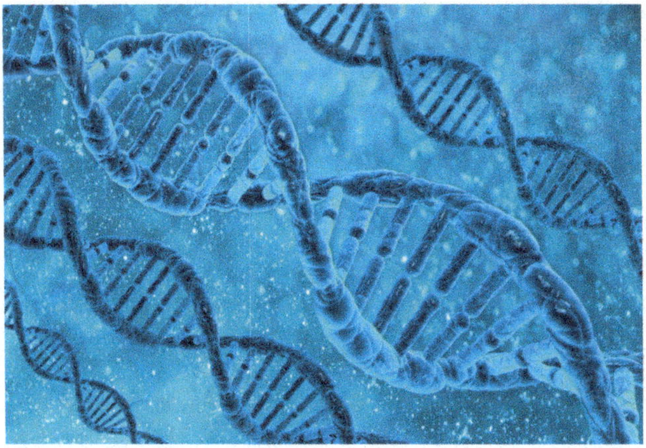

Benefits of a Healthy, High-Energy Environment

There is an important saying, "The most important ability is availability." When I operate with great energy and focus, I am significantly more productive in every facet of my life. Combine this with never being sick or missing a day of work or school and you can see how productive I have been over the decades. If every member of a company or organization has high energy, enthusiasm and focus while rarely missing a day, you can imagine how this will affect your bottom line. Add a high level of communication that builds relationships, and a healthy, desirable culture will grow.

You will also achieve two massive benefits:

- Better retention and recruitment of executives and the workforce.

- Improvement in marketing for new clients and members.

Massive validation of these benefits exists. Their boost to the bottom line is significant. For example:

"I was simply amazed when we focused on the health, energy and mental focus of not only the employees but the leaders of our high-tech company. Our profitability rose 23 percent in the next quarter. We also had a significant increase in applicants for all positions. I suspect this was because our workforce enthusiastically referred highly qualified, good people our way. For this success, I have to thank an all-inclusive wellness program, which identified and worked with our weak areas and the workforce."

P. Nigel

Tying It All Together

Working with Vital 100 Wellness will have a massive positive effect. We can transform an organization or business from unprofitable to highly profitable, from an undesirable place to work to one that is quite desirable, with a workforce skilled in communication so that every member of the workforce and your executives, will grow from "just working for the boss" to highly passionate and empowered, individually and collectively. Spread these cultural and personal improvements over everyone in a company and the "global" benefits will be observed immediately.

Our team will work with your organization, company or team to make sure your bottom-line results will improve and be capable of being maintained. Our highly skilled group will not only effectively take your company or organization to another level, but we all "practice what we preach." That makes working with a group so much more predictable and more easily translatable. The following statement embodies this concept:

"You cannot take someone to where you have not been."

This distinguishes our program from other similar programs, e.g., our diversity and the fact that we embody what we teach and coach. If we are not skilled communicators or are not healthy, high-energy people, how can we help your company, team or organization soar?

Our program is not only groundbreaking in what we offer, but is highly effective and customized to your organization's needs. What we coach and teach is validated through multiple studies and research. Many studies have shown that a team, corporation or group will perform at a much higher level and achieve more significant goals when each member is energized, focused, and has developed the skills to deliver at a higher level.[2] When a group, company or team comprises highly energized and focused members while being coached and well-directed, their potential is unlimited.

---

2 Abby McCain, "22 Telling Employee Wellness Statistics [2023]: How Many Companies Have Wellness Programs," Zippia 22 Telling Employee Wellness Statistics 2023 How Many Companies Have Wellness Programs Comments (Zippia, March 1, 2023), https://www.zippia.com/advice/employee-wellness-statistics/.

We can guide your organization through the difficulties of incorporating and maintaining the qualities that high-performing, highly effective groups utilize to become the best in their fields.

In the next chapter, I detail how health affects performance. By implementing these concepts, you can transform your company. I encourage you and your company to aspire to be not only highly competent but the best in your field. Our goal is to assist you on that journey.

Chapter 2

Wellness: How Health Affects Performance

Performance is how well you do your job and the results you achieve, whether as a CEO, company owner, employee, or athlete on a team. Performance can range from a poor showing (not achieving a goal or regressing backward) to an acceptable performance to an optimal performance and outcome. Obviously, the closer to optimal a team or individual performs will bring that person, their team, or company closer to exceeding previously established goals.

If a majority of members of a team, company, or organization can achieve optimal performance, the more optimal the overall goal achievement will be. Achieving lofty goals has its own motivating energy. The question then becomes, "How can you help a majority of members achieve optimal individual performance so that the company, organization, or team collectively can achieve an optimal result?"

One critical point here is that if a majority of individuals in a group achieve optimal performance, they must be coordinated and directed to be moving toward the same goal. Teamwork on a sports team (no different from any other team) is critical to winning a championship, as opposed to a collection of superstars all selfishly trying to reach for individual but uncoordinated success. The coaching program we have with Vital 100 Wellness not only creates high-performing individuals, but individuals who are well-coordinated in their journey to achieve their lofty goals and collective success.

Health and wellness are often poorly understood by business people, while health professionals and researchers are often unaware of the nuances of business and the effects of health on business, as their filters are through their expertise in health.

As the name implies, corporate wellness blends the areas of health with business. For a program to be successful, the broad areas of business and health must blend seamlessly so each area will enable the others, rather than function independently.

True health and wellness have many aspects when considering how they affect business or performance. Brain chemistry must have a full complement of balanced neurochemicals (acetylcholine, serotonin, GABA, dopamine and more). The brain must be continually cleansed and nourished (occurs at night with deep healing sleep). These conditions are critical for optimal cognition, focus, overall health and hormone balance. The brain is the true control center of the body.

For the brain to function optimally, nutrition, proper stimulation, stress reduction, supplementation, and the state of the working environment are immensely impactful. Other areas critical for overall health include hormone balance (this includes the stress hormone cortisol), energy production, weight management, transmissible infection prevention, detoxification, elimination and more.

Business Functions Affected by Subpar Health

The following are areas of a business function that less than optimal health or inevitable health challenges individually or as a group will affect:

1. Lower energy by individuals (workforce or executives) will lower their production capacity.
2. Preventable absenteeism (many reasons, most of which are preventable) will decrease production.
3. Imbalanced brain chemistry affects energy, hormones, focus and creativity.
4. Preventable headaches and other pains will take away a person's focus from work. Most pain issues are preventable or easily resolved.
5. Addictions such as sugar, drugs, smoking, alcohol and more all negatively impact production and performance.
6. Poor nutrition or lack of nutrients negatively affects every system of the body.

7. Compromised sleep negatively impacts performance and focus.
8. Preventable illnesses remove a person from the workplace for extended time frames. Many long-term illnesses have an obvious impact on a company's or organization's bottom line.
9. Poor stress management strategies or systems are critical for performance.

An optimal corporate wellness program, as the above examples demonstrate, will positively impact or minimize all these potential performance distractions in executives and the workforce. When a team member within an organization or a company "is down" or compromised, there is a ripple effect throughout the organization. It may affect the corporate culture, stress levels, or overall wellness when even one person is absent or compromised.

That is why a top corporate wellness program is an important investment for the corporate culture and the group's bottom line. Depending on the business focus, our program, corporate wellness plus communication effectiveness training, will yield a return of between $6 and $12 for every dollar invested.[3]

Jennifer Schaefer, writing for the Rand Corporation (The Real ROI for Employee Wellness Programs, Feb 2015) has shown a $6 return for every $1 invested in wellness programs.

---

3 "What's the Hard Return on Employee Wellness Programs?," Harvard Business Review, August 1, 2014, https://hbr.org/2010/12/whats-the-hard-return-on-employee-wellness-programs.

Energetics International has published studies (The ROI of Better Communication Skills) that highly effective communicators (internal and external communications) will increase a company's bottom line by 47 percent.

These two programs combined within Vital 100 Wellness are critical in yielding between $6 and $12 for every dollar invested.

Top 10 Research-Based Benefits of Corporate Wellness

1. Each member of the workforce will experience improved health indicators.
2. A wellness program will prevent or mitigate lifestyle diseases.
3. A wellness program will improve the emotional and mental health of employees.
4. Healthcare costs will decrease far more than the cost of a wellness program.
5. Absenteeism due to injuries, stress, bullying, depression and disengaged employees is reduced.

   Better employer branding and improved recruitment: 87 percent of applicants consider a wellness program important when applying; 67 percent like their job more when they have a wellness program, and 45 percent would stay on their job longer if their company utilized a corporate wellness program.[4]

4 MS Debra Wein, "Council Post: Win with Wellness -- Attract and Retain Talent," Forbes (Forbes Magazine, August 29, 2018), https://www.forbes.

6. Corporate wellness increases productivity company-wide.
7. Wellness programs increase creative thinking.
8. A wellness program improves team dynamics, job satisfaction and employee engagement.
9. Wellness programs also increase team cooperation, a better sense of community and better interpersonal relationships.
10. Add to a wellness program for corporations, groups and teams a program of communication enhancement and developing a performance mindset and the improvements will be palpable.

Areas of Focus

Each company or organization is unique, requiring different approaches from our work with each client. The parameters for how and to what extent we work with them will determine how we customize their program. While there are many similarities from one program to another, there will also be distinctions.

The following will need to be determined before we structure an organization's program:

- Their goals and desired outcomes.
- The size of their company.
- Length of time requested to work with an organization.

---

com/sites/forbesbusinessdevelopmentcouncil/2018/08/27/win-with-wellness-attract-and-retain-talent/?sh=6b946ea61648.

- The services we provide to the organization.
- The depth of the work we provide. the organization.
- The budget of the group with which we are working.

An initial discussion will help us determine the structure and cost of our services. Anticipated outcomes will be a critical factor when designing an organization's program. Although customization of a program is critical (this makes our program distinct), as described above, the program with Vital 100 Wellness will address three general areas. Each of these areas has been well researched and demonstrated that they maximally influence the bottom lines of organizations and each individual within the organization.

As a side note, the bottom-line results for a company or organization are truly the sum of each individual's progress and performance multiplied by a factor of at least two. This makes sense because synergy, teamwork and an improved corporate culture will raise a bottom line far higher than the sum of each individual's improvement.

The three general areas of focus we work with companies and organizations are:

- **Corporate health and wellness:** This is much more than traditional parameters of health and addresses the deeper health of a person to genuinely affect their longevity, energy, mental and emotional outlook and ability to focus.
- **Communication skills:** Effective communication is promoted within an organization and to its customers or clients.

- **Performance mindset:** Helping members of an organization develop a performance mindset accelerates a person's contribution to the organization.

Each of these areas of focus individually will greatly impact the bottom line, while synergistically, the results will be magical. A company or organization can choose the services from any of the three areas, but we suggest designing a program that addresses all three areas simultaneously. Each program is synergistic with the other two.

If executives, the workforce, or leaders are healthy, energized and more focused, this will positively affect their communication effectiveness. When all members of an organization or company can communicate with a positive mindset, stress management, focus, energy and overall health will reach optimum levels.

These three areas of focus were intentionally selected because of their substantial individual impacts on your bottom line. However, they mutually enhance bottom line outcomes more than each of these areas individually.

The corporate health and wellness component will assess and work on each person's health and energy levels before focusing on any other area. We have found that this order of coaching optimizes each person's ultimate productivity. In addition, working with the enhancement of communication skills will improve each person's ability to raise their productivity and the productivity of everyone with whom they interact.

Together, the three areas of focus will achieve and even exceed the goals your organization aspires to achieve.

Mitigating Health Conditions and Stresses

As an owner, president, or CEO, the bottom line and overall performance are a good benchmark for how the entire enterprise is performing. Various factors collectively contribute to the bottom line and performance, including production or service quality, effective marketing efforts and budgetary considerations.

Few realize the equally important yet somewhat obscure factors affecting the group performance and bottom line: the health of every individual within your company or group. There are several factors encompassed within health—physical, emotional, and mental—that if even one person in a company is affected or absent, the productivity and bottom line will be negatively impacted. Fatigue, addictions and seasonal infections (e.g. the flu season) or epidemics are easily mitigated circumstances, which I will discuss in more detail in the following sections.

1. Fatigue

Fatigue (physical or emotional) is one of the primary considerations. Whether one person, a department, or an entire company or team is affected, fatigue can be very debilitating. Many factors affect the mental and physical energy levels and thus the ability to perform and contribute optimally.

One's mitochondrial (energy factories in every cell) health and function will greatly determine the energy available for each cell and, ultimately, the person. Many factors impact mitochondria function, such as nutrition, thyroid health, overall lifestyle, toxicity and stress, all of which are treatable, yielding more energy while decreasing fatigue.

Mental fatigue affects one's ability to focus and think for extended periods. The brain is truly the conductor of so many of the body's functions and overall performance.

Toxic buildup, nutrient absences, low energy production, and inflammation from trauma or infections are the factors that will affect the brain and its performance. When caught early and prevented or mitigated (the right approach can catch brain stressors early), the brain will continue functioning at a high level. The result is excellent productivity, well after most contemporaries are noticeably fading or have lost optimal brain function.

2. Addictions

Addictions are another negative factor affecting individual and organizational performance. Addictions take many forms and are quite prevalent in the general population. Depending on the addiction, the amount of compromise to a member, company or team will vary.

Common addictions include sugar, particular foods, alcohol, smoking, gambling, recreational drugs, sex and pharmaceuticals, to name a few. Each of these addictions will compromise an individual's or a group's performance in varying amounts. The difficult part of addiction resolution is first to identify the addiction and generate motivation to do the work to resolve that addiction.

The easier part of addiction resolution is to treat the underlying or root causes of addiction, which are generally nutrient imbalances (usually, this appears as a deficiency). Then, simultaneously, balancing the major brain chemicals, which include serotonin, dopamine, acetylcholine, GABA, norepinephrine, histamine, and glutamate, will produce the best results.

A program to identify and treat the causes of addictions will have a tremendous result on the overall performance and bottom line of companies, teams and individuals.

3. Seasonal Infections and Epidemics

Widespread sicknesses, such as influenza (flu) season or the recent COVID epidemic, disrupt a company, organization or team. Many within the workforce or team are forced to miss daily work activities because they cannot function well enough and want to avoid spreading contagious viruses to the rest of their team.

The fact that these disruptors are because of viral spreading is both a problem (easily passed to others) and an opportunity. It allows us to mitigate or eliminate these viral infection disruptors. One may think that influenza or Covid vaccinations are the answer to reduced individual and group infections. However, there is much controversy about the efficacy and safety of vaccines. Several doctors (Frank Shallenberger, December 2020 letter and Joseph Mercola) continue to sight studies which are at odds with NIH and the CDC. There are no definitive answers to whether vaccines are the best way to prevent these viral infections. I have six friends, family and doctors I have worked with that have been negatively impacted by the vaccinations and two of these who were healthy have died within weeks of receiving them.

Although I am not against vaccinations, there are more direct and effective prevention or treatment strategies of these infections I recommend. These involve regular disinfection (three to four times per day during highly contagious times) of the entry portals (eyes, nose and mouth) for viruses with immune enhancements, using vitamin and herbal therapies, healthy lifestyle choices, such as more sleep and avoiding sugar and other immune lowering consumables. Prevention of viral infections is more effective than treatment of full-blown illnesses and certainly contributes to more effective maintenance of a "healthy bottom line."

Tying It All Together

A health-savvy wellness program is critical to prevent or mitigate other health and performance challenges. These include:

- Mental focus or ADHD.
- Disruptive nutrition, which causes a broad range of health effects.
- Multiple chronic illnesses.
- Accelerated accident, trauma, and surgical recovery
- Gastrointestinal disruptions: the GI system is where health begins.
- Finding alternatives to most disruptive drug prescriptions.

A company does not have to feel like illness and its effects on optimal performance are just the "luck of the draw." The approach to health, performance and success should be proactive and, as a result, will profoundly affect the bottom line.

An effective corporate wellness program, combining groundbreaking research with a health-oriented approach instead of an illness approach (or one that just medicates symptoms) will be most effective at preserving the bottom line and helping any company, organization, or team accelerate its success. Effectively improving health and wellness promotes a better corporate culture, the glue that holds your entire organization together.

Chapter 3

The Glue That Binds Your Organization Together

Your corporate culture is the glue that holds your company together. The bottom line and their overall compensation motivate the owners, administration and even the stockholders. Even though they are motivated by a paycheck and occasional bonuses, the workforce is truly excited to come to work where everyone is working toward the same goals and feels comfortable and passionate about working as a team.

The cinematic phrase that embodies a productive and effective corporate culture is "All for one and one for all." What factors produce a corporate culture with collective compassion and affinity to work with others on the team and for the benefit of the organization, company or team?

The first factor is that everyone will benefit when the group does well, not just a select few. When individuals in the workforce and above them on the organization chart feel that their interactions (within the group or to the outside) will be appreciated and rewarded, they will put in the extra effort to have their collective group be successful.

Training in communication, work skills, work habits, and product and service knowledge demonstrates to the workforce that the owners and administration care about every individual. Celebration of success and achievements is also critical in developing a positive, nourishing corporate culture.

Developing Care in Corporate Culture

Much research has validated that when those at the top of a company or organization take a genuine interest in all within their group, company or team, all members feel they are essential, not just replaceable pieces. [5] This sends the message of "We care." When they feel cared for, all humans

5 Christine M. Pearson and Christine Lynne Porath, *The Cost of Bad Behavior: How Incivility Is Damaging Your Business and What to Do about It* (Toronto: Portfolio, 2009).

realize their true potential, and their efforts will generally come forth.

Why create a corporate culture that fosters goodwill and encourages all to perform optimally? The following reasons should confirm the importance of a nourishing corporate culture.

- Better retention and improved recruitment.
- Lowered stress throughout the company or group.
- Improved overall health of every individual.
- Significantly less absenteeism; less need for medical services.
- Everyone works more productively; they don't just try to "get by."
- Every member will be encouraged to give positive, honest and productive feedback.
- Every facet of what goes into the bottom line will be enhanced, resulting in overall greater success.

A good or poor corporate culture starts from the top down. For example, an arrogant, uncaring and selfish CEO, owner or director will create and foster a hostile, unproductive corporate culture, while a caring, insightful, positive leader will build a productive corporate culture with an equally healthy bottom line.

A company experiencing only modest uncivility and hostility will have lost work time, weakened commitment, reduced work efforts and even people who left the company due to a poor corporate culture generally manifests from the top down.

It was calculated in *The Cost of Bad Behavior* by Christine Pearson and Christine Porath that one highly regarded health care company lost almost $71 million as a direct result of incivility and their uncaring corporate culture.[6]

It is then apparent that an investment in an owner, CEO, or director to develop areas of communication, their own health, and even counseling to improve their understanding of interpersonal relationships and motivations is critical for a thriving corporate culture to develop.

The status of a group's, company's or team's corporate culture is not easily measured as with income or new clients, but the development of the corporate culture is instrumental to a group's short- and long-term success. The development of a positive corporate culture should not be ignored. The ability of leaders to gauge the status of their corporate culture is done through periodic interviews, occasional surveys and informal, honest discussions with members of the workforce. If individuals in the workforce trust their leaders with whom they are discussing how they perceive the corporate culture's status, they will be open with honest feedback. Negative and positive feedback are both valuable for different reasons. We all like positive feedback, but more importantly, negative feedback should be used to grow and improve corporate culture and the entire organization.

---

6 Christine Pearson, Christine Porath, and Warren Bennis, in *The Cost of Bad Behavior: How Incivility Is Damaging Your Business and What to Do about It* (New York: Portfolio, 2009), pp. 37-40.

Ignoring the health of the corporate culture within a company, group, or team will be detrimental to its success. Ignoring the corporate culture is done at your peril !

Customization

Although most organizations will exceed even the loftiest expectations through enhanced wellness and communication skills, the value of working with Vital 100 Wellness rests on its customization. Each organization is different in size, the types of individuals we would work with, and the ultimate goals desired and envisioned.

Flexibility is also critical and is something we focus on. If, after we begin our program, goals and what types of services are necessary to achieve the goals changes, we will recalibrate and potentially restructure our program. The ultimate goal is to achieve and even exceed an organization's target goals. Customization and flexibility are critical to reach those goals expediently. Approaching a goal is never a straight line direction but is a series of course corrections to more quickly and effectively arrive at the goals.

Customization and flexibility are inherent styles that Vital 100 Wellness "brings to the table" in working with your organization. If a company or program proposes a bottom-line enhancement program, customization and flexibility must be an integral feature of that program. Additionally, a program that effectively enhances each member of your company MUST address these three areas:

- Wellness
- Communication
- Performance

Collectively, these will skyrocket your bottom line. However, if these features and programs are not part of the overall program you're considering, your results will not hit your goals. Although our program is highly effective, being efficient and respectful of an organization's resources (time and finances) will always be how we approach work with our clients.

Implementation

The most incredible ideas, strategies and goals will just remain ideas unless the plan or program is implemented. Once the plan and goals for an improved bottom line have been approved and the plan comes together, it must be implemented or much time and other resources will have been wasted. Implementation and how this program will become a reality must actually be its own plan, independent from the initially planned program.

Before implementing a plan or a program, several aspects must occur. The first is to bring together the tools necessary to achieve the goals of an organization. These goals must be fleshed out.

1. What does an organization want to achieve regarding its bottom line? Their operating principles and their culture must all be considered.

2. Are these plans viable, given the budget, existing workforce and executive mix?
3. How do we customize the tools to achieve their stated goals?

The next items to bring to the table before implementation are the costs, necessary space and time frame available to achieve their goals.

Implementation Tools

What first tool is needed before beginning the work with Vital 100 Wellness? Once we realize we can achieve the goals and the plan (including resources and time frame) is ready to initiate, then implementation begins.

Implementation begins with an assessment of the workforce and executives as well as a time frame. Here are several issues that will be learned during individual discovery if our work will work with each individual within an organization:

1. What are their individual goals?
2. What percentage is overweight or unhealthy?
3. How motivated are the executives and the workforce to learn how to become more productive?
4. What are the pre-existing health status and communication skills?

Once these issues are clarified, a plan will be formulated, including a time frame for how to customize this plan. Within this plan will be:

1. The services of the plan.
2. Time frame to impart this information, strategies and practices until they are incorporated.

The sequence of teaching each part of the plan is critical. There are several components that must follow others. For example, before a weight loss program can be put into practice, nutrition and certain lifestyle concepts must precede initiation of that program.

Working with individuals will usually follow group coaching sessions. It is important to reiterate that implementation will vary greatly with budget, components of each company's overall program and time frame.

Observable Change

An important part of implementation is the space dedicated to the program and the time during each day, week, and month dedicated to the group and individual corporate wellness and communication skill training pursuits. It is important to understand that observable improved productivity will bypass the cost of this program. It will also become evident that company time dedicated to this program will be more than compensated by increased production.

For example, it may take several weeks or months for observable production increases to become apparent. We have had companies and organizations notice a change and positive results almost immediately, but this varies from group to group and depends on the agreed time we will work with a company or organization. Nevertheless, it takes time to instill new lifestyle habits, effective communication skills, and an optimal performance mindset. The time you invest in your program will ultimately determine how quickly change and bottom-line improvements are observable.

Example during Covid Pandemic

The value of combining wellness and communication was on display with a small recruiting firm. Not only were they going through the Covid isolation, but their inability to communicate within their company was obvious.

Our program first focused on Covid protection to get people back to work, allowing enhanced communication skills to be developed. Not only did improving communication skills work to decrease stress but allowed for improved teamwork followed by increased sales. This demonstrates the combined effects of a wellness program with coaching in communication skills. The different aspects of this program were customized for this recruiting firm and were well coordinated. Once the components of our program are agreed upon, we put together the corporate wellness and communication skill training sequence for implementation and then initiate the program.

Because each person in the company is critical to the success of our work, an individual consult with each person will usually be the launch of our work. Once we understand where the collective group is beginning, it will be much easier and, ultimately, more effective in reaching the organization's goal. Because each group we work with will have a customized program, initial private or small group sessions will be essential and scheduled when they will be most effective.

Regular updates for individuals and the entire group will be critical and will be provided. Progress must be measured and feedback must be given to all. We are certain that every individual, their families, and the leaders and CEOs will become acutely aware of positive progress in their bottom line and how they feel and function.

It is both an intent, desire and expectation that the work of Vital 100 Wellness with your group be a win-win-win for all involved. Your satisfaction and positive results are what we strive to achieve.

What Is Success?

As the CEO, owner or leader of your company, organization or group, you have focused your energies on making your dream and company a reality and a success. For most, being a success translates as:

1. Financially profitable.
2. Creating a functioning environment, aka "corporate culture," where people enjoy working, creating and being part of a successful "venture."

To most leaders, this means getting more products and services "out the door." For most, this is measured by looking at the bottom line and seeing a profit without consideration of how they arrived at that profitability. The concepts introduced in this book will make a huge difference in the lives (and bottom line) of everyone in your company, their families and the lives of your clients and customers.

Tying It All Together

Having a successful wellness program is the key to skyrocketing your bottom line. More important is having one mapped out direction and guide on how to reach bottom-line results by improving the performance of everyone in your organization by improving the health, energy and focus while raising everyone's communication and operating skills.

It is important to realize that few companies or organizations know that the power of higher energy, passion and health, combined with high-level communication skills, will take their business to much higher performance levels. Training, coaching and health enhancement, such as we offer at Vital 100 Wellness, will be your company's superpower.

The results of working with us will create an incredible shift within your organization while positively affecting every person your workforce and executives touch. This includes families, friends and customers. Almost indirectly, your bottom line will explode exponentially as a manifestation of a healthier, more engaged workforce and executives.

In summary, implementing an effective corporate wellness program as we offer will result in:

- Greater individual and organizational energy.
- A better-focused workforce and executive-level leadership.
- Less absenteeism and decreased healthcare costs.

- A more desirable corporate culture.
- Improved retention and recruitment results.
- Decreased overall costs for operating.
- More sales of products and services.
- More robust marketing.
- More effective communication internally and externally (B2C).
- Everyone will feel a part of this organization's vision.
- Improved overall performance by all members at all levels.

The next chapter discusses performance. So, with all this to gain and nothing to lose, what are you waiting for? Are you ready to fire up your rocket?

Chapter 4

Wellness: The Fundamentals

The expression, "You cannot take someone to where you have not been" couldn't be more true. How can anyone take your company to health and productivity if they are not healthy and productive themselves? I realized many years ago that by being optimally healthy, passionate and high- energy, I could achieve many goals that most could not achieve. Working out daily, being an Olympic trials qualifier, being a health innovator, avoiding illness for over 50 years and "walking my talk" in health, energy and focus qualifies me to take people to a level of optimal health and productivity.

In addition to a high level of personal health and fitness, my partner works with athletic teams to help them achieve a high level of performance. His many accomplishments, instructive events and innovations also allow him to add a tremendous amount of value to the companies and organizations we work with. His performance work allows athletes and top people (CEOs and leaders) to acquire the skills to reach greater levels of accomplishment.

We have the collective knowledge and skills to raise others to levels of health and performance they have never experienced.

Categories of Health Practices

Two categories are considered for individual health practices. The first category is healthy fundamentals, basic health practices for everyone to become healthy, energized and focused. These fundamentals include:

- Basic nutrition (what to eat and what to avoid).
- How to best sleep for daily healing and renewal.
- Incorporating physical activity.
- How to decrease stress and anxiety.

Each of these four areas includes many strategies and ways to achieve excellent health.

The second category of health practices has to do with customizing each person's individual health needs. Differences in genetics affect variations in health for each person (only identical twins have similar genetics), lifestyle differences, different approaches to stressful situations and our individual environmental exposures.

Some of the more common reasons people differ in their health status include:

1. Genetically, many people are poor detoxifiers, while some are robust detoxifiers of toxins.

2. Mold-infested houses, autos or places of work are immense challenges to overall health. Some of the sickest people are exposed to daily mold. There are also many other environmental and closed-space toxins that affect health.

3. Poor diets (e.g., high-sugar or inflammatory foods), lack of physical activity and underactive thyroid glands will lead to major health issues. These are issues that can be easily controlled by those individuals experiencing these challenges.

4. Infected root canals can lead to many complicated health challenges. Detecting these infected teeth and treating them will have profound changes to people's health.

5. Toxic air and water are two of the most significant health challenges to which a large part of our population is exposed.

6. Poor sleep (for varying reasons) will lead to hormone disturbances, cancer, fatigue and poor daily performance, to name a few.

These are just a few reasons healthy energy levels and focus will vary from person to person. Our work with organizations, companies and teams will not only assess fundamental health challenges each person must resolve, but we will show them how to be optimally healthy so they can incorporate ongoing "healthy practices," resulting in reduced illness and optimal performance.

Variations in our health program to your group will also be determined by how involved we become. Additionally, the motivation of the individuals we work with will vary. We realize that not all individuals are optimally motivated to become healthier or perform at a higher level. However, even owning a small part of our work will raise all members to a higher level of health, energy, focus and overall results. In other words, if most individuals in a group can raise their level of performance even 10 percent, the overall bottom line will improve dramatically. We strive to raise the average performance of each individual by at least 25 percent.

Determining Underlying Factors

Besides teaching healthy fundamentals, Vital 100 Wellness has cutting-edge tools to identify the underlying factors that result in fatigue, illness, lack of focus and low productivity, and exactly how to eliminate them. The critical concept to help individuals (workforce to executives) become highly productive, energized and focused is to have their bodies and minds functioning optimally. The way to do this is to identify and remove the obstacles to health, energy and mental function while providing the tools the body needs to function like a "well-tuned machine."

Examples include removing infections and toxins while providing the correct nutrients and building blocks, compensating for genetic weaknesses, and instilling healthy mental patterns.

In addition, utilizing new technology that is simple, cost-effective and non-invasive is raising people's enhanced performance to previously unimagined levels and reversing their aging. Reversing aging alone raises performance and enthusiasm many levels higher.

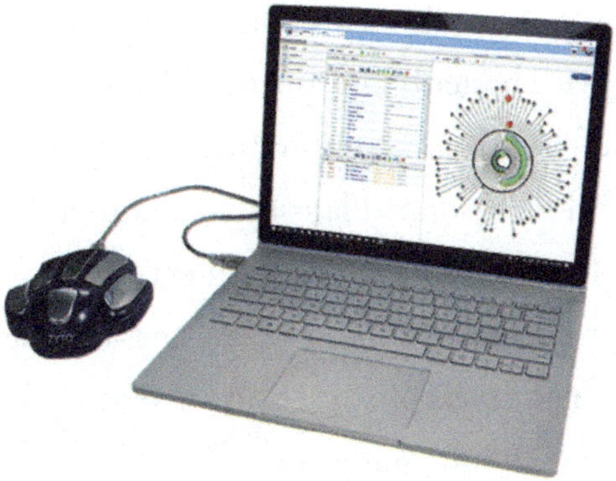

Our program assists individuals in healing themselves to reach a level of optimal function and health. Masking symptoms to achieve artificial health, such as using one or more of many categories of pharmaceuticals, is not only a poor and ineffective approach to achieving top performance, but is frustratingly temporary.

Vital 100 Wellness is prepared to help each individual within your organization, company or team achieve this level of optimal health and performance. If the majority of members in an organization, company or on a team perform at a much higher level, the entire group will elevate its bottom line to levels not thought possible.

How Does Wellness Affect Performance?

When every team, organization or company member raises their ability to focus and improves their collective energy, passion and cognitive function, the entire entity will rise as well. The phrase "a rising tide raises all boats" comes to mind.

It is important to agree on the term "wellness." Wellness includes resistance to illness and having higher energy while functioning with better brain function. Unfortunately, these parameters of health are compromised in a toxic environment (this will be described later), poor nutrient intake and assimilation (the Standard American Diet, SAD, is very detrimental to wellness), poor lifestyles, and lacking physical activity with high levels of stress and anxiety. Each person is affected by these in different ways.

Nevertheless, health originates because of several basic functions in the body. These critical questions affect health:

- Do we have every nutrient and element our body needs for optimal wellness?
- Does our body remove the toxins and wastes to which we are exposed internally and externally, or is the accumulation of toxins compromising our health?
- Do our cells produce the necessary energy (ATP produced by the mitochondria) for healthy functions (e.g. digestion) and observable daily functions, such as exercise?

How well is your brain functioning given the stored memories and toxins within the brain to which we are all exposed? Wellness and performance have a direct and intimate relationship between them. The healthier, more energized, and more focused you are, the more productive you will be. Production is being able to complete tasks, assignments and projects with high quality in a timely fashion. Production is also completing these tasks, assignments and projects consistently over a significant period. Consistency, while being available, is a critical part of productivity. No one is able to be productive if they are not well, focused and have high energy over a longer period.

A metaphor for production is that it is a long-distance race rather than a sprint.

The final part of productivity is that group productivity is a team effort, not just the collective performance of each individual. That is why communication skills and performance mindset training are critical to overall productivity. These areas of our work with an organization focus on improving teamwork. We will discuss communication skills and performance training as integral components of productivity and, ultimately, bottom-line results.

Collectively, a person (individually and as part of a group) that is healthy, has high energy and focus, possesses good communication skills and understands what goes into optimal performance will be very productive and an integral component of a high-level corporate or group culture.

How Corporate Wellness Affects Overall Performance

It is critical to understand how each basic area of health and productivity (aka an improved bottom line) are related. Thousands of chemical reactions in our body proceed second by second. Each reaction requires certain nutrients to function properly. If the nutrients (oxygen, magnesium, proteins, electrolytes and more) are missing or depleted, those reactions either do not occur or are compromised. The resulting end product (e.g., improved energy, digestion, detoxification, allowing the brain to function or get restful sleep) will not operate efficiently. This results in lower energy, poor nutrient uptake, a buildup of toxins, slower brain function, or increased anxiety due to poor sleep.

It is easy to see how each of these basic functions will compromise a person's productivity and, thus, a company's or organization's bottom line when spread across the workforce or within the leaders and administration. The special and unique effectiveness of Vital 100 Wellness is that we utilize tools to detect health compromises quite early in their disruption to correct them easily. Early detection and correction of health functions and problems help every member of an organization to smoothly and effectively function without disruption. This also includes our work with addiction resolution or mitigation.

To illustrate this, if a member of a company or organization contracts cancer, has a heart attack or debilitating illness (the Vital 100 Wellness team can usually identify years before and help to resolve them), this person will avoid downtime and a disruption of the company, organization or team. Resolving illness quickly is also valuable in mitigating an organization's collective downtime. For example, mitigating downtime for athletes or company leaders helps keep them playing or directing without interruption.

One of the significant benefits of corporate wellness is avoiding or lessening downtime.

Tying It All Together

The concept of health prevention or early intervention applies to individuals, companies, organizations and teams. Identifying functional and cultural problems early in a company or organization will be much easier to correct, resulting in future cost savings and productivity interruptions. Identifying health challenges within the workplace is a great place to start, which we will discuss in the next chapter.

Chapter 5

The Working Environment: Profound Health Challenges

Many factors affect how a team or individual performs. Communication skills, an individual's health and the various components of each of these areas will greatly affect an individual and company's performance and as a result the bottom line. One of the least understood factors significantly impacting how a team, company or organization performs is its working environment.

One's performance will be impacted every minute by lighting, air quality, noise levels, circulating infecting microbes (e.g., Covid) and working ergonomics on each individual. The working environment is so critical because it affects every occupant all day, every day they are in that environment.

The quality of the environment will affect not only every one of the senses but also the brain, digestion, hormones and the immune system. Additionally, even subclinical environmental stresses will increase our body's cortisol (the stress hormone) levels, which in turn negatively impact every tissue and system of the body.

A number of years ago, the Environmental Protection Agency (EPA) had to close down for months to work on their own mold and toxic air remediation as the air quality was compromising every person in their offices. If a government agency focusing on the environment could not detect how toxic its own working environment was until many workers became deathly ill can you imagine how other companies and organizations fail to monitor their own environment and continue to operate with compromised workers oblivious to their health and performance challenges.

It is estimated that more than 50 percent of the homes and work environments in the US have water damage leading to mold toxin exposure, a health compromising or even a deadly exposure.

Air quality is critical, as is light quality. Blue light being emitted by computers, TV's and hand- held devices compromise eyes and brain function but can be easily mitigated with sensitive diagnostic tools and effective technology.

People sitting at their desks for hours will compromise their structural alignment and immune systems. Over time these stresses will cause absenteeism, compromised performance as well as reduced energy and overall operating enthusiasm. In extreme cases of compromised structure (pain issues) and immunity, hospitalization can result. These are best avoided with simple preventive measures as provided in an effective corporate wellness program.

Mitigating working environmental stresses will be one of the most critical programs to incorporate into a company, team or organization's facility and working environment.

Communicate Effectively and Civilly For Maximal Results

An interesting story came from my conversations with the surgical team members at a large hospital. The head of a highly respected surgical team was a doctor who was abrasive while interacting with his team members and patients. Although he was technically skilled and achieved good surgical outcomes, he disrespected and verbally abused his team members. His team turnover was quite high, and his abrasive style offended many of his patients, who stopped referring clients to him despite his surgical skills.

Although his team members were reluctant to bring this to his attention, the hospital put him on probation, subject to that doctor working with a counselor to revamp his attitude and communication skills. His team remained unchanged; however, within six months, they were viewed as a model surgical team because the team leader (that doctor) changed his communication style and attitude. He came to understood how important effective, civil communication was for the overall team's success and how critical his new communication style was in reducing operating stress.

Both verbal and non-verbal communication is critical for success in one's personal life and within businesses, organizations and teams. Effective communication will positively or negatively affect all those around you and will be a significant factor in your performance in life and business. Additionally, it can transform a poor or average-performing company into a highly profitable, blockbuster company when multiplied over all members of a company, organization or team.

Not only is effective communication good for business outcomes, but effective civil communication profoundly affects the mental, emotional and physical health of all members of a business group or team.

Success in Business Communication

Business success through good communication and the health of the workforce are interchangeable. Effective and civil communication will dramatically improve the health, attitude and performance of everyone in a company, organization or team. When you have healthy individuals in a group (this is the focus of our corporate wellness program), they will be better, more enthusiastic communicators and have the energy to become optimal performers.

Healthier, more energized people are more enthusiastic and better communicators (both within an organization or company and to its customers), which creates a thriving corporate culture. A good communicator with enhanced communication skills contributes to a healthier corporate culture. Combined with a robust, customized corporate wellness program, the leaders and workforce will quickly become healthier overall.

Civil communication directly improves the corporate culture, leading to a successful business or organization and healthier people. Healthier people lead to increased energy within the organization and eventually to a more successful business. Health, the corporate culture, and a robust bottom line are intimately related. Ignoring employee and administrator health and the corporate culture while focusing solely on the bottom line will be much less successful than what your bottom line could be.

The biggest cause of stress in the workplace is uncivil, poor relationships initiated and perpetuated by poor communication. The American Psychiatric Association has estimated that workplace stress and anxiety cost the United States economy more than $500 billion per year, resulting in 550 billion work days lost and greater than 70 percent of workplace accidents.[7] It has been estimated that a majority

7 "Stress in America: Paying with Our Health," American Psychological Association (American Psychological Association), accessed February 4, 2015, https://www.apa.org/news/press/releases/stress/.

of doctor visits are related to stress. Stressed workers have healthcare costs that are 46 percent greater than less stressed workers.

Other ways workplace stress affects workers, and thus the bottom line, are:

- Forty-eight percent of workers intentionally compromise their work effort.
- Forty-seven percent intentionally decrease their time at work.
- Thirty-eight percent decrease in the quality of their work.
- Eight percent lost work time worrying about stressful situations.
- Sixty-three percent lost time avoiding stressful offenders.
- Sixty-six percent said stress negatively impacted their performance.
- Sixty-eight percent said their commitment to the company lessened.

- Twelve percent left their job because of stressful relationships.
- Twenty-five percent took out frustrations from stress on their customers.

It has been calculated that top firms (Fortune 1000) spent 13 percent of their work time (7 weeks in a year) dealing with bad employee relationships.[8] Poor relationships usually emanate from poor communication. Poor communication interferes with problem-solving and program implementation. These issues increase stress, resulting in poor worker retention, health challenges and the inability to improve critical functions within a company, group or team. We commonly observe poor communication leading to poor relationships and unnecessary stress within underperforming organizations.

Poor workplace performance emanating from ineffective and uncivil communication can take several forms. Uncivil communication is generally not malicious but comes from the lack of understanding or ignorance of what constitutes poor communication and how it affects production and, ultimately, the bottom line.

8 J. Connelly, "Have We Become Mad Dogs in the Office?," Fortune, November 28, 1994, https://archive.fortune.com/magazines/fortune/fortune_archive/1994/11/28/79988/index.htm.

Identify Bad Communication

Expressing anger or hostility when talking with others in the organization is the first and most obvious form of bad communication. Usually, hostile communication comes from displeasure at a perceived poor outcome. This negatively impacts the receiver of the hostile feedback and spreads it to other group members. As an example, if a team within a larger company is led by a generally angry supervisor who regularly expresses hostility (or does not praise others when appropriate) before, during, or after the day the day's work is compromised, more mistakes are made, support staff generally does not want to work on that team, and the health of the entire team (due to stress and anxiety) suffers.

In an interview I did, a supervisor in a company routinely gives negative performance reviews, always finds fault in most circumstances with others in that department, and never gives compliments. More than 70 percent have given their resignation or were considering resigning. As a result, the department director had to offer almost 20 percent higher compensation to entice applicants or keep those working in that hospital department. This is directly a result of uncivil communication and low emotional intelligence (EQ) from the supervisor "in charge." The solution would be to either find excellent communicators, especially when searching for supervisors, who can form good relationships or are open to developing effective and civil communication skills.

Hostility or generally angry communication is where communication will obviously compromise outcomes and overall health, but there are also forms or examples of poor or improper communication which affect outcomes and, by extension, the bottom line. Other forms of ineffective communication are chronic or diffused throughout the group, small or large.

The following are more subtle examples of poor communication actions that eventually undermine and destroy a group. Collectively, these will bring about devastating results if not identified and corrected:

- Neglecting to say please and thank you.
- Use of email when face-to-face is necessary.
- Taking most of the credit for a collective work effort.
- Emailing or texting during meetings.
- Keeping people waiting inappropriately.
- Talking down to others.
- Delaying access to information and resources.
- Using jargon or foreign language to exclude others.
- Passing blame when you are part of the problem or mistake.
- Spreading rumors and gossiping.
- Belittling others verbally or non-verbally (rolling eyes, smirking).
- Shutting out someone from a team or network.
- Taking advantage of others on the team.
- Showing little interest in others' opinions.
- Not listening.

- Showing up late for meetings or leaving early without explanation.
- Insulting others in private or public.
- Failing to acknowledge others and their efforts.
- Demeaning or directing derogatory remarks to someone.
- Taking others' contributions for granted.
- Grabbing easy tasks while leaving difficult ones for others.
- Forgetting to include others.
- Speaking unkindly of others.
- Sending uncivil or rude emails.
- Behaving disrespectfully when disagreeing with others.
- Interrupting others when they are talking.
- Avoiding looking out for others.
- Judging people who are different, based solely on that difference.

These are all examples of uncivil communication that undermine an otherwise nurturing, effective culture. Identifying the communication disruptors and providing the tools to eliminate them, then substituting civil, effective communication tools is what we focus on to help companies incorporate. This will positively affect the health of every person in your company or organization and reboot your corporate culture and, ultimately, your bottom line.

Techniques to Enhance Communication

Civil, effective communication will help to develop a healthy, nurturing corporate culture, which will raise the bottom line. The following outline shows the goals and benefits of effective communication.

The Fundamentals

- Shows respect for all.
- Solves problems and moves forward with dialogue, which engages all members.
- Establishes operating norms that must be regularly followed.
- Considers all involved in operations, including the critical workforce, administration, leaders and customers.

The beginning of optimal communication is the fundamentals. Each person in an organization must practice these fundamentals for effective communication skills to develop.

Optimal Communication

- Saying please and thank you will develop kind, warm and sympathetic relationships.
- Lead with a smile and a helpful attitude to begin all communication positively, which spreads to others. Smiling has been shown to increase the immunity and health of the sender and the receiver.

- Build relationships with subordinates. This has been shown to engage others and signal they are cared for.
- Listening: true listening signals caring, commitment and connection. When employees see they are being heard, they will be more inclined to contribute ideas and suggestions that improve operations. Asking others what they think will engage employees at all levels.

Critical Practices

When promoting and teaching optimal communication after the fundamentals, the following are critical practices to develop a culture dedicated to team growth and the overall bottom line.

- **Share resources:** tools, knowledge, social contacts and time. These acts promote better relationships and increase motivation among all.

  It has been shown in a variety of industries and businesses showed that the greatest performing companies and teams shared more resources, including feedback and purpose. This also included sharing knowledge, their time and contacts.
- **Share recognition:** with all who contributed (being humble and allowing all who worked on a project to be recognized). This promotes better engagements, more satisfied members, and higher retention.

- **Share gratitude:** increases self-worth and confidence, builds greater trust and a desire to help others.
- **Share feedback respectfully: share feedback about** personal performance and organizational performance of positive and negative outcomes. Sharing feedback increases a sense of ownership, increasing the bottom line. Shared feedback should be within a safe space where negative and positive feedback is still comfortable.
- **Share purpose:** this promotes growth, engagement and a sense of well-being. Overall, sharing of purpose builds relationships, improves the corporate culture and, finally, the bottom line.

Tying It All Together

The fundamentals and more advanced techniques in which communication thrive are critical to developing an organization, business and team in that everyone excels, wants to become an integral component and will positively affect every member. Incivility in a group, organization or company begins with poor communication, leading to decreased production and a compromised bottom line.

Two studies investigating the connection between communication and productivity showed that uncivil communication led to compromised mental agility, fewer cognitive resources, decreased attention and overloaded working memory for people subjected to incivility.[9] Subjects in the studies exposed to incivility were 30 percent less creative and had 25 percent fewer ideas for problem-solving. Additionally, clients subjected to incivility became less helpful or were less inclined to assist others on their team. These studies validated incivility and inappropriate communication's negative impact on compromising productivity.

Investing in communication training had significant positive effects on a team's outcomes and positive effects on the workforce's overall health. Now that you know the techniques needed, it's time to implement them.

In the next chapter, I discuss implementing and maintaining these techniques effectively.

9 Christine Porath and Christine Pearson, "The Price of Incivility," Harvard Business Review, January 2013, https://hbr.org/2013/01/the-price-of-incivility.

Chapter 6

Effective Implementation

No potentially effective program will be successful unless implementation is part of the strategy. Implementation consists of several components. All must be included or overall implementation will be unsuccessful, regardless of how passionate the implementors are or how effective the program is.

Implementation begins with understanding what goals a company, organization, or team wants to achieve and the motivating factors to reach those goals. This will take several discussions and a bit of homework by the decision-makers. The more developed companies, organizations and teams may include other members as an inclusive, culture-building activity. Once the goals (realistic or moonshot-reaching goals) have been established, an assessment of the organization and its members will determine the attitudes and motivations of those involved in achieving those goals.

An organization, company or team with many members who have negative attitudes or those wanting to maintain the status quo at all costs will have an arduous journey to improve overall performance and reach the desired goals. Constructing a plan to reach a company's goals must take all the gathered information to develop a customized program for your organization to reach those goals in a timely manner.

Our experience with different groups and organizations is that the most effective programs for developing skills and overall wellness must involve people from every level of an organization (workforce up to top management and owners). When every level of an organization feels they have input into this program, they will be more invested in the implementation and its overall result. This ultimately leads to a quicker and more effective pathway to achieve the initially agreed-upon goals.

Techniques for Achieving a Company's Goals

These are ten of the most effective ways to develop effective and civil communication within a company, team or organization. Effective communication will not only help the development of a highly effective corporation, but it is critical to developing highly productive client relationships. This generates sales for immediate and long-term results.

1. Group talks.
2. Individual consultations.
3. Individual or departmental reviews and assessments.
4. Individual health assessments.
5. Programs to develop healthy, high-performance routines.

6. Online lessons.
7. Lifestyle assessments.
8. Follow up.
9. Communication workshops.
10. Work with leaders.

Truly "connecting" with clients will stimulate not only long-term business connections, but also referrals. It's apparent that outstanding communication within a group and with its clients will help all aspects of the business. What is not as well understood is that effective relationship-building communication is good for the health of every member of the workforce. It reduces anxiety and stress and will help companies and organizations in their retention and recruitment efforts.

Studies have shown that well-honed, caring and civil communication are good for business and the health of everyone in that organization, resulting in reduced operating stress and improved outcomes.[10, 11]

Civil Communication

A case illustrating the importance of civil communication saw a manager interact with a highly effective, experienced

---

10 Natalie Slopen et al., "Job Strain, Job Insecurity, and Incident Cardiovascular Disease in the Women's Health Study: Results from a 10-Year Prospective Study," *PLoS ONE* 7, no. 7 (July 18, 2012), https://doi.org/10.1371/journal.pone.0040512.

11 Getty Images, "Workplace Stress: Your Co-Workers Might Be Killing You | Head Case," The Wall Street Journal (Dow Jones & Company, August 20, 2011), https://www.wsj.com/articles/SB10001424053111903392904576512233116576352.

and respected supervisor with a lengthy critique in front of his team that "he was not doing his job." The manager also ignored this supervisor's response to the criticism. Uncivil communication can profoundly affect others, which can cause retaliatory responses. The next day, the supervisor called in sick (that had never happened before), which rendered his entire team non-functional and unproductive for that day. This resulted in significant productivity loss for the company.

A productive company, team or organization invests resources in developing civil and constructive communication skills as a critical step toward a well-functioning team that consistently achieves its goals. Education strategies, including group presentations, individual consultations, and numerous education tools, will develop business and communication, which is good for business. Brainstorming, repetition and individual studying of effective communication for all aspects of your business will quickly develop the skills necessary to skyrocket your business.

I was involved in a health clinic with a receptionist who displayed anger while continually blaming others for any problem she had. She also attributed most complaints about her to racist people within our clinic. When she was ultimately released, she took her complaints to two regulatory boards despite her complaints having no actual basis for them. The resulting actions eventually consumed tens of thousands of dollars in legal expenses and hundreds of manpower hours and resulted in unmeasurable stress to our health clinic.

This is a classic example of how disruptive one person with poor personal and communication skills can damage a company or organization and why each person should be coached in both health and communication skills within a nurturing corporate culture set up for optimal outcomes.

It is important to realize that not all members will be on board to develop their communication skills and improve their health. Therefore, it is critical to identify these people who are unwilling to work on themselves to advance the group and organization and decide if they will continue to be "on board." Do we ignore them, try to convince them, or let them go from your team? Having resistant people will lower a company's eventual results.

It is truly amazing how successful, simple and transformative it is when you have 100 percent participation to achieve the company's goals. Techniques and tools utilized by Vital 100 Wellness to educate a company, organization or team are critically important to achieve a healthier bottom line and a healthier corporate culture. These are not tools and skills that fall in the lap of an organization. They must be presented and coached. Developing healthy routines and high-level communication skills takes time, but it is well worth the effort and time necessary to incorporate them into the corporate culture.

Habits and Routines

Routines: Sequence of actions that are regularly followed.
Habits: Regular tendency or practice, especially one that is difficult to give up.

I commented to my brother on a three-day family reunion that being thrown out of my daily routine from my familiar living situation was difficult. Lacking a familiar routine disrupts regular sleeping, eating, exercise, daily flow and supplementation pattern.

My routines have been developed over the years to maximize my energy, comfort and daily accomplishments. Not only does a well-developed routine maximize what we accomplish, but so much of a daily routine is on autopilot, which serves to help optimize your day's accomplishments while decreasing stress and anxiety since so much is done with little or no thinking. Unfortunately, many people have fallen into unhealthy, lazy routines and habits which accomplish little or, worse, can be damaging or counterproductive.

It can be quite difficult to deprogram those with unhealthy and unproductive daily routines and habits.

Routines are quite valuable if they are healthy and productive. However, unraveling bad or unhealthy routines by oneself is difficult. This is where highly accomplished coaching is Important. The coaches can identify from their viewpoint "above the fray" what habits (regular tendencies) and routines are being practiced day-to-day or hour-to-hour and give guidance on how to correct them before substituting habits and patterns that are actually healthy (group wellness) and eventually become highly productive.

In the 80s, I was a national class runner who independently developed with little outside coaching. As a practicing doctor, I had many other activities and responsibilities on my plate other than athletics. I knew I had natural talent as a runner, but had never participated on a team or had a coach, so I did not know what I could accomplish. I coached myself through much research and many hours of practice.

Nevertheless, my best teachers were the mistakes I learned, and because I had lofty goals, I was motivated to learn from these mistakes and find time for training. What I also realized in retrospect was that over a two- to four-year time frame, I developed an amazing training routine in which every day of the week had a particular phase of running and fitness. Over three years, I could gauge my progress without any disruptive variables. With my weekly routine in place, I quickly advanced from an above-average runner to a national-class runner who qualified for and ran in the Olympic Marathon

Trials in the mid-80s while being ranked 35th for the marathon in the US.

I learned that by identifying and correcting bad habits as part of an evolving, successful routine, I could achieve several lofty goals even greater than I could have envisioned initially. Although I am no longer a national class athlete, I still evolve my health and professional performance within my daily and weekly routines in healthy and experiential ways, allowing me to accomplish many goals. I continue to learn and develop many new skills and businesses while helping and coaching others to achieve their goals, which I attribute to successful habits and routines.

Pushing beyond one's comfort zones while maintaining the fire of curiosity is critical to becoming the best person or group one can be. These qualities will always make life exciting. I use my experiences (personal and educational) while observing the experiences of others to develop advanced wellness programs for individuals, groups and organizations.

The Importance of Good Routines and Habits

Routines comprise of several smaller habits. Both habits and routines can be healthy and productive and move us closer to our goals, helped by a longer vision. On the other hand, routines and habits can be destructive and unhealthy and move us (an individual, organization or company) further from desired outcomes and goals. The wrong metrics, personal filters or measuring tools can easily guide any of us in the wrong direction.

Expert coaching can help to establish a desirable endpoint and develop the steps, habits and routines to reach desired goals or endpoints. We acquire habits and routines because of familiarity and because our minds and bodies more easily repeat an activity for which we are rewarded. This reward can be emotional, mental, or physiological, intended to avoid pain or move toward our perceived goal. This is typical of pharmaceutical, drug or sugar addictions, which reward us (makes us feel good) but have extremely deleterious long-term consequences. Breaking these destructive habits requires substituting healthy activities for destructive ones.

Moving counter to an established routine or breaking a habit takes more energy and usually becomes more mentally and emotionally uncomfortable in the short term. For example, breaking out of a sugar consumption habit or starting an exercise program to lose weight or prepare for a race is very difficult, even if we are aware of how difficult it may be during the transition.

An individual or company, organization, group, or team that desires to achieve several ambitious goals must realize these goals are composed of smaller goals and actions. Some of these smaller goals and measures may move us closer to the ultimate, desirable goal, and some actions may run counter to achieving that goal. Actions not helping us move toward the ultimate goal should be discarded. Individuals and organizations must be careful in setting goals and seek assistance to set production goals. This assumes that the ultimate goal is productive and truly a desirable endpoint.

How a Program Can Help

A coaching or consulting program, such as Vital 100 Wellness, realizes that determining the ultimate goal or endpoint is where to begin the process. These goals may be measured purely by numbers, such as the bottom line, the number of new clients or something less definitive, such as developing an ideal corporate culture. Nevertheless, establishing the ultimate goal is where the process begins. Even though the process begins with setting the end goal, that goal can move as we approach it. An experienced outside consulting or coaching group greatly assists in setting these goals because of their experience and utilization of advanced assessment tools. A good coach or consultant also brings another set of "eyes" to the process.

Once the end goal is established, a series of steps or intermediate goals (usually with timelines attached) will serve as benchmarks to monitor the progress toward the ultimate goal. Keep in mind that the ultimate goal will also evolve during the process of working toward that goal. This is actually desirable as long as the new goals are not shifted significantly downward.

It is much easier to visualize intermediate progress when the ultimate goals are broken down to a series of manageable steps or smaller "bite-size" goals. When the smaller steps are determined, the hard work begins. Reaching even smaller goals requires identifying what habits and routines are being practiced consistently every day, week, and month by a majority or, ideally, every member involved in achieving that particular goal. The more productive and healthy habits practiced by more members in the organization or team, the quicker the ultimate goal will be reached.

Once the routines and habits are identified, it is critical to reinforce good habits and alter or dispose of bad habits and routines that interfere or slow progress toward the ultimate goal. Unproductive habits and routines should constantly be identified and assessed to make sure they are aligned with the ultimate goal.

Tying It All Together

If an important member of an organization or company repeatedly attempts to work while recovering from frequent hangovers, health-compromising eating habits and lifestyles that reduce their energy levels by 50 percent (not uncommon in our population), it will decrease overall production. Multiply this by a majority of the workforce or executives, and the bottom line will suffer dramatically.

When not civil, or if not enhancing others, communication skills directly or indirectly sabotage lofty goals. Moreover, they will surely result in a deteriorating corporate culture, which decreases the health of every involved individual.

Goal achievement and overall productivity are not unlike an assembly line or the function of an automobile. When one step in an assembly line is dysfunctional, the negative impact will quickly spread to the entire assembly process. The assembly line will either stop or the resultant end product will be of much lower quality. This will have its effects felt throughout the company or organization.

If an automobile has a poorly functioning part in the engine or electrical system, that automobile will break down prematurely. Likewise, in business, if one member of a company or organization is severely compromised, it will eventually negatively affect the entire organization. The more critical the compromised member is within an organization, the more significant and quicker the negative impact on the production and the company or organization.

Most compromises in a group, company or team emanate from unproductive health and lifestyle habits or damaging uncivil communication skills. These can be quite obvious to trained consultants and coaches outside an organization, but may be challenging to identify from within the company or organization, as these habits have become part of a daily routine that appears normal from within an organization.

Similarly, identifying unhealthy, damaging habits and routines usually requires special skills to uncover and develop strategies to eliminate them. The longer these unhealthy, unproductive practices, habits, and routines persist before identifying and eliminating them, the more difficult it is to replace them and the longer it will be to achieve a stellar bottom-line goal.

Chapter 7

How to Identify and Eliminate Unhealthy, Unproductive Habits and Routines

Author Rita Mae Brown coined the phrase, "the definition of insanity is doing the same activity repeatedly and expecting a different result."[12]

Common health and lifestyle issues that undermine achieving goals or sabotage the bottom line are:

- Low energy: most people can increase their energy levels.
- Chronic pain.
- Regular absences or sicknesses.
- Poor motivation.
- Negative thinking or pessimism.

12 Rita Mae Brown, *Sudden Death* (New York, NY: Bantam Books, 1988).

- Poor family dynamics.
- Anger issues.

Experienced coaches and wellness programs are critical for assessment by using different eyes to identify where, who and how the destructive process is undermining not only individuals but teams, organizations and companies. Destructive, unhealthy, or unproductive individuals or groups within a larger group are generally not intentional activities but poor communication skills emanating from truly unhealthy people.

The process of identifying each individual's contribution to the bottom line can start with a single unit or individual within a department or smaller groups. Once identified, these smaller "units" can be taught productive communication and how to truly be healthy, high-energy and better aligned with the organization's larger goals.

Individuals who do not "get it" or are unwilling to change their actions, communication or health (mental and emotional) may be moved out of the company or organization. This is the call of the CEO, owners, executives, or managers in charge, who, hopefully, realize how difficult individual "speed bumps" can have far-reaching effects throughout an organization or company.

Once unproductive people's actions have been identified, instilling good habits and routines comes into play. It is quite easy to develop good habits and routines once you identify where and with whom they should be inserted. The difficult part is usually how to change an individual's unproductive but ingrained habits and routines. To be successful at these changes is where a combination of education, practice, and, if all else fails, soft threats come into play. It makes no sense to have individuals or small groups within a larger company, organization or team negatively impacting many others or the entire organization with their unhealthy energies and uncivil communication. This is especially pertinent when these negative issues can be corrected or improved with good assessments (corporate wellness) and excellent coaching (communication skills).

As my own history proved, developing good habits and routines will take individuals to extraordinary levels of joy, health and production in a relatively short time frame. When an entire group or company raises its energy and production levels to previously unimagined levels of production and joy, the entire group will easily reach its bottom-line goals and desired corporate culture levels.

Creating a Flourishing Environment

To make a body of water (pond, lake or river) a top fishing destination, the water is periodically stocked with fish that will flourish and spawn. If that water is polluted or devoid of oxygen and nutrients, the fish will either die or not be able to reproduce, resulting in a poor fishing destination. The same scenario occurs in companies, organizations and teams. If there are bad employees, executives, or members within an organization, due to any number of reasons, that organization will eventually die or yield a shrinking bottom line, no matter how exceptional the product or service.

Ongoing work on these fundamentals (wellness, effective communication, and focus) is incumbent upon the CEO, owner and other influential executives who want to maintain a healthy company or organization and effectively ramp up production and their bottom line. Even though many CEOs and executives will solely focus on product development and marketing initiatives, they may not embody health and wellness or utilize effective communication styles, and their company's bottom line will negatively reflect these shortcomings.

To walk the line of health, energy, focus, and passion while leading with good communication, CEOs and leaders must continue to learn and develop personally, and disseminate these skills and qualities throughout their organization. This is done with a dedication to learning and evolving within their position and to insist the growth of skills and work-enhancing qualities is incentivized and embraced by all. It is not enough to have a passionate, high-energy CEO with excellent communication skills and not have the workforce embrace this mindset.

A workplace employing a workforce that is not on board with continued enhancement of health, communication skills development and utilization of a high-achieving performance mindset critical for an evolved company will open itself to undermining, sabotage, lack of dedication, and an inability to retain or recruit good people. This ultimately leads to a sluggish bottom line, long-term struggles or even failure. The conclusion is that developing healthy fundamentals is critical for this type of evolving organization and must be ongoing.

Laying the Foundation for Success

- First, CEOs and executives must be on board with a program to enhance their health, passion, energy, focus, and communication skills.
- Next, it is important to see who is open to this growth in the workforce. For those who are not, a choice must be made to reward or let a person go who is unwilling to strive for individual and teamwork growth within the company or organization.
- Finally, creating growth opportunities and coaching for the entire workforce will have the biggest positive impact on the overall culture and the bottom line. Not only will everyone be more productive through an enhancement program, but when every company, organization or team member understands how important they are to the company's results, they should be more passionate and invested. This ultimately translates to bottom-line success with pervasive happiness and satisfaction.

Wellness and Performance

Wellness and performance are intimately related. Without health (short or long-term), high energy, and focus, your performance will suffer dramatically. In interviews, I have talked with employees and leaders who admitted their ability to perform was compromised by greater than 50 percent or more when they had headaches, were exhausted, were going through severe PMS, or just had poor focus.

Performance is even more compromised when a group's members depend on drugs, caffeine, or other artificial enhancements to achieve even average results. Although athletes are identified and punished for using performance-enhancing substances such as steroids, artificial performance enhancement is also common at every level of society, usually with undesirable personal and group results.

Vital 100 Wellness works with individuals to enhance health, energy, and performance in more natural ways. Most of our clients can minimize or eliminate their use of drugs with healthier products, lifestyle changes and our addiction resolution program. Most drugs (recreational or pharmaceuticals) compensate for natural brain chemical deficiencies that can be assessed and provide alternatives. This will help to eliminate or minimize the need for performance-enhancing drugs (prescription or illicit drugs) and caffeine boosts while helping those addicted to smoking.

Anxiety and Stress

Anxiety and stress are among the least recognized destroyers of performance (along with overall health). Stress can result from internal sources (poor diet, poor detoxification) or external sources we all experience. The approach to decreasing stress and anxiety is through expert coaching. Reducing stress and its compromises on performance involves three strategies:

1. The first is to identify external sources of stress and to minimize them. This includes eliminating bad relationships, poor sleep practices while learning to say "NO" when saying "YES" would increase stress.

2. The second is to learn how to react to the outer world and its attendant stresses by letting many of these stresses "pass you by." This skill is learned with a properly trained coach and effectively reduces daily stress. When you understand this method to reduce stress, you realize that most of the communication

and external stimuli we encounter are meaningless and that letting it "pass you by" will bring great mental and emotional peace. Effective communication is an integral component of this second step for eliminating or diffusing much potential stress.

3. The third way to decrease stress and improve health and performance is to physiologically identify how you react to stress (the stress hormone is cortisol). Hormone balancing, specific stress-reducing technology, and increased detoxification go a long way toward maintaining health, even in stressful situations.

All three areas of stress management are critical to optimal health and performance. Stress is endemic within groups attempting to improve their bottom line and performance and is best managed with a wellness program utilizing more natural strategies rather than talk therapy or anxiety-reducing pharmaceuticals.

Many components impact performance within groups (composed of one to thousands), and your bottom line will skyrocket by addressing as many as possible with an eye toward long-term results. Your job as a CEO, president, manager, captain, or leader is to improve your group's performance. Improving every individual's performance will achieve an improved bottom line, and that improvement will far outpace any previously established goals. This is the approach Vital 100 Wellness uses to help your group and its collective performance.

You can address the usual parameters of your company, organization or team performance. At the same time, your wellness program gives you the tools and strategies to enhance your bottom line, a healthier, more passionate workforce, enhanced communication, better sales and a culture that raises every component of your business or team.

The McKinsey Quarterly, which surveys companies throughout the world, has noted that top publicly traded companies (top quintile) have shown a three-time return to stockholders and an 18 percent productivity improvement when a company incorporates a wellness program.[13] It has also stated a strong and static correlation between improved corporate wellness and financial performance. The companies that showed the most improvement were lower-performing companies when a wellness program was initiated.

A February 2015 survey of more than 500 business leaders across the United States in various industries and company sizes noted that healthy focus and wellness programs positively affected morale, engagement, and overall corporate performance.[14] In addition, a majority of these business leaders felt that an effective wellness program was a critical investment in their human capital and their company.

---

13 "Organizational Health Index," McKinsey & Company, accessed December 16, 2022, https://www.mckinsey.com/solutions/orgsolutions/overview/organizational-health-index.

14 "Business Leader Attitudes about the Role of Health as a Driver of Productivity and Performance ," Exploring the Value Proposition for Workforce Health (Health, Productivity, and Performance Study Committee , February 2016), https://www.shrm.org/ResourcesAndTools/hr-topics/benefits/Documents/HPP-Business-Leader-Survey-Full-Report_FINAL.pdf.

Finally, business leaders felt that a wellness program positively affected their company's direction, innovation and learning, leadership, coordination and control, capabilities, motivation, work environment, accountability and external orientation.

Tying It All Together

You are the business owner or leader and want to prevent backsliding from healthy habits and routines or move your group forward or faster. You may feel that a new business plan, improved marketing or hiring new more stellar people are the answers—to some extent, that can help.

Unfortunately, when the critical basics are dysfunctional, you cannot put your foot on the gas, and your company, organization or team will not magically move forward or accelerate its positive evolution. Tremendous research has shown that highly skilled civil communication is critical for the accelerated, sustained growth and health of an organization or group. Developing these skills takes time and skilled coaching. Once installed, practice is necessary to become habits that will take a company or organization to exceptional levels.

Healthy members with energy, passion and focus are also critical for positive, sustained growth. Unhealthy lifestyles within the workforce or in executives will spread throughout an organization or company like a virus. Low energy, lack of passion and poor focus will also immediately manifest in the bottom line and performance of all. The process begins with the CEO and executives embracing a program to strengthen, enhance and grow their organization. Once embraced, they commit to not only their own development but that of their workforce and team.

Our customized program is available for companies, organizations and teams in every niche and any size. It will greatly benefit all groups and, by extrapolation, every individual and their families. All that is necessary is to commit to a program of health, communication enhancement and the development of a performance mindset.

Chapter 8

Case Studies: The Value of Health and Performance

Although it has been described, studied and dissected in many ways, your health does affect your performance (personal and professional), mind, and, ultimately, your bottom line. The following case studies further illustrate how these are intimately related and affect each other.

The Power Couple

A husband and wife saw me present an online talk on several health concepts in 2020 and wanted me to work with them on their health. He is a college administrator, and she works for an IT company. They both felt run down and were taking several medications they wanted to stop. They wanted a more natural approach, not the pharmaceutical approach they were on, but did not know where to begin.

After a distant health assessment (we have the technology to assess health at a distance), I altered some of their lifestyle choices and nutritional makeup. I had her visit a biologic dentist to eliminate several infections and her toxic fillings. Within two to three months, they both had significantly more energy. He lost 25 pounds, and she lost about 45 pounds.

I continue to work with them to maintain their health, which is the envy of their family and friends. He has begun several new educational programs in the past year, and she has revamped her department within her IT company. Because of their health successes, they have referred over 15 clients with whom I have achieved many clinical successes and many positive testimonials. In some sense, my work with this husband and wife has positively affected their community as they are well connected and continue to refer people to me while they share those health concepts they now practice with those in their sphere.

The Sales Representative

A US sales representative for a German contracting company was a client of mine. Her main concern was that she was 45+ pounds overweight, and with her family's history of obesity, dementia, and cardiovascular disease, she was rightfully concerned. Because the main concern was her excess weight, we began a comprehensive, health-oriented weight loss program.

In six months, she lost 52 pounds and has kept off the pounds with new eating and lifestyle choices. More importantly, her sleep was better, her energy noticeably improved, and her overall mood and focus had also noticeably improved. She showed significant improvement in a follow-up blood test compared to past years. Because her clarity and confidence had improved, she was able to close several large contracts for her company within four months of our wellness work together. This earned her a significant bonus and raise. She is quite grateful and attributes much of her success to our overall health work together.

The Athlete

One case involved a runner who had reached a frustrating two-year plateau with his marathon times. Because he regularly became injured, interrupted training prevented him from improving his times. He learned about my health and performance work from a fellow runner.

I helped him with his nutrition and sleep regimen and corrected several of his stretches. I also introduced him to innovative, effective relaxation and stress-reduction strategies. As a result, within six months, he improved his race times in the marathon by over 12 minutes, propelling him to win the competition within his age group consistently. We can attribute much of this to keeping him injury free.

Working with athletes is similar to working with others who desire to achieve significant life and professional goals, and it is the same with leaders and directors of companies.

Tying It All Together

Once a CEO, owner or executive has decided to invest in their company's growth, it is time to take action. Here are a few critical decisions before pursuing a program to move your company, organization or team forward:

- How involved should my company, organization or team become to enhance the skills, performance and the health of all our members or employees?

- Who should be involved? (Executives, workforce and far-reaching contacts within our company or organization.)
- What are our potential goals and what level of bottom line and culture do we want to achieve?
- What is the time-frame necessary to achieve our goals? (Short-term, long-term or somewhere in between?)
- What are the financial investments we want to make?
- Which programs can offer whatever goals and achievements we desire?
- Is a customized program important to us and our organization?

It is critical to realize that all corporate wellness programs are not the same and their effectiveness will differ. Your results will vary depending on what each program offers and the people involved in implementing this program. One critical question of a consulting group to consider is: "Do the people within that group walk their talk and can they convey that message and motivate that group?"

Many programs are just based on traditional health parameters such as weight and blood pressure measurements. These programs do not consider the underlying cause of issues such as weight gain, loss of energy and focus, poor sleep, chronic illness or unrelenting anxiety. Groups simply utilizing time tested health parameters only will not achieve long term, high performing results.

Finding the underlying causes of illness and low productivity, as measured by the bottom line and corporate culture buy in, while helping to correct them by giving participants the tools, knowledge and motivation is a much more highly effective approach. The environment in which people work is also critical to health and productivity. This is where communication skills and the health of the environment (many environments are unhealthy and contribute to lower productivity) are so critical.

As a result, a program which works with overall health, communication skills and performance mindset is what will yield desired results quickly. Once the skills and knowledge are provided, long-term maintenance will occur. Understanding the offerings and details of a corporate wellness program that focuses on individual performance and how that translates to bottom line performance is what makes the wellness program of Vital 100 Wellness valuable.

Collective individual health, focus, improved lifestyle enhancement and communication skills plus group synergy will yield high-level improvement of your bottom line and group performance.

Postface

Final Words and Key Takeaways

How the Wellness Program Delivered by Vital 100 Wellness Is Different

Once wellness and productivity interrelatedness can be understood, it is easier to conceptualize the importance of maintaining wellness and how to appreciate what Vital 100 Wellness actually does. Our traditional health care system is very adept at treating acute problems such as a fracture, laceration or other acute health issues. They are also good at intervening with late-stage disease, which needs immediate, invasive intervention. This includes late-stage Alzheimer's or late-stage IV- Cancer.

Unfortunately, these acute issues with invasive intervention are rarely needed in dealing with wellness and performance. When traditional allopathic medicine gets involved with chronic health issues or enhanced performance, the approach is to mask symptoms. These are symptoms such as chronic pain, fatigue and hypertension. Treating or mitigating symptoms temporarily reduces those symptoms (decreasing pain, normalizing blood pressure, stimulating adrenals for more energy) but does not resolve the issue causing the symptoms. The health issue or illness will eventually return if symptoms are only masked. Pharmaceutical intervention rarely eliminates the underlying issues of an illness or health problem and more often creates multiple side effects.

The preferred approach by Vital 100 Wellness is to find underlying causes for illness or compromised performance and correct them. Usually, alterations of lifestyle choices while giving the body the tools to heal itself will dramatically improve overall health problems and enhance performance. The results of our patients illustrate this very point.

- High blood pressure is usually resolved with magnesium (a frequently deficient mineral), kidney cleansing and blood vessel dilation. All of these are easily done without medications and will generally last for a lifetime. Pharmaceutical treatments of hypertension are accompanied by a myriad of side effects.

- A woman suffering severe depression is effectively treated by administering a highly effective amino acid combination, broad spectrum vitamins and deficient neurochemicals. In a high percentage of situations, this will resolve the depression in several days.

- Acid reflux (heart burn or GERD) should not be minimized with antacids or Proton Pump Inhibitors

(PPI) but can usually be resolved with digestive enzymes and hydrochloric acid, which together will also enhance nutrition absorption.

- Low energy is generally a function of a poor energy-producing mechanism in the body. Stimulants will increase energy in the short-term but are accompanied by dangerous addictions and other illnesses. Special natural products and some lifestyle changes will dramatically increase energy in the long term.
- Effective weight loss with lifestyle changes (coaching necessary here), decreasing anxiety and better nutrition will dramatically enhance health, longevity and energy for the long term.
- Reducing inflammation using natural products, decreasing anxiety and better nutrition will improve energy, heart and brain health, pain and immune resistance. This translates to a reduction in absenteeism and better performance.
- The brain is very sensitive to anxiety, infection and environmental toxins, such as mold in the work or living spaces. These cannot be treated effectively without understanding brain function and balancing brain physiology while delivering overall health coaching.

These are just a few examples of how Vital 100 Wellness is different in its approach and dedication to long-term health and wellness. Our programs are generally simple, healthy and low-cost. When learned, they can be practiced for a lifetime and even extrapolated to family and community. This approach is why we get widespread acceptance and continual referrals.

Using groundbreaking assessments and treatment approaches delivered by health practitioners who practice what they advise others is an effective approach. The wellness and performance program for a company, organization or team is a practical approach to increase the bottom line.

Areas Vital 100 Wellness Addresses

A deeper dive into the arena of health affecting productivity and performance is important to understand how intimately the two are related. If you have experienced overwhelming fatigue, brain fog, lowered motivation, a lack of passion, or are sick with the flu so you can barely function, you can then understand how health compromises affect your production. Many people with less severe health compromises still attempt to "go to the office" or work in a compromised state, and their work is still compromised. Chronic illness, fatigue or lack of focus will affect many people in a company, organization or team. This is why Vital 100 Wellness is so valuable. No one functions at 90 percent or more all the time, and many within a group will just go through the motions regarding their daily responsibilities.

Vital 100 Wellness will not only raise the collective passion but decrease absenteeism, help each person raise their energy levels, focus, and communication skills. Spread over an entire workforce and within administrators, this will collectively raise the bottom line dramatically. We use cutting-edge technology for assessments, lifestyle counseling to individuals and groups, highly effective, natural products and more.

Conditions that Vital 100 Wellness treats which will directly affect performance:

- Low energy levels.
- Depression.
- Chronic brain dysfunction.
- Diabetes.
- Improved sleep.
- Chronic pain.
- Communication skills.
- Performance blockages.
- Prevention of Covid, influenza, and seasonal allergies.
- Inflexibility.
- Workplace illness.
- Post-meal brain fog.
- Chronic illness prevention.
- Mitigating health emergencies and absenteeism.
- Much more, as it relates to health and productivity.

Mitigating or preventing these problems will raise each member's performance and positively affect the company's, team's or organization's bottom line for the long term. Our practitioners include health-oriented naturopaths (natural doctors), manual therapists, nutritionists, performance counselors, advanced-degree health practitioners and communication and relationship counselors. These practitioners will not only deliver their expertise to members and leaders in your company or organization but orient their work to improve performance both in your group and in the individual lives of your team.

This will have a positive impact on their life's passion and their professional work. The positive energy within every individual will resonate with the group's culture. I know that this is a special gift Vital 100 Wellness brings to each company, organization, team or group to raise the Energy resonating within a group. The difference between having passion and a desire to perform at one's highest level versus the feeling individuals have to work to earn their paychecks is two completely different levels of performance.

Integrating our other areas of expertise—raising communication through civility—will be the glue that binds every individual together. There are volumes of research that validate how improved wellness and enhanced performance mentality create a highly functioning culture in which the company, organization or team works toward one mission. Combining this with enhanced communication skills raises the overall bottom line, surpassing all goals and measurable parameters. The excitement of what can be is very observable and, more important, is possible.

The Components Constituting Performance

The combination of reaching a goal (specific bottom line goals, number of enrollments, winning a game or championship) and how it is reached comprises performance. Reaching a goal involves goal setting, a time frame to reach that goal and the necessary steps. These should be set before embarking on the process or updated as you progress. Vital 100 Wellness can assist in setting a goal (must first know the history of the company, organization, or team) because we will know what our teaching (corporate wellness, communication and instilling a performance mindset) is capable of doing with the participants. Nevertheless, as the team or organization progresses, we also will assist in goal recalibration. Goal recalibration must consider:

- How Vital 100 Wellness can alter performance.

- What the company, organization or team brings in terms of knowledge and history of the members, their products, services and their culture.

In terms of performance, here is what Vital 100 Wellness can influence and what we work with:

1. **Energy and focus of members:** special technology and knowledge can dramatically increase the energy and focus of every member.
2. **Improve wellness and decrease illness:** early detection and prevention will decrease absenteeism and dramatically decrease illness while accelerating healing.
3. **Increase excitement and passion:** motivation increases on the way toward reaching a goal.
4. **Increase group retention:** as a result, this also improves recruitment.
5. **Increase sales:** better communication skills improves sales.
6. **Improved communication within an organization, company or team:** this decreases mistakes, allowing more team synergy.
7. **Decrease the costs in many areas:** this will directly improve the bottom line.
8. **Positive word of mouth will spread:** communities will notice and spread the word.

9. **Improved skills and better operational knowledge in many areas within an organization, company or team:** this is a critical component of a constantly improving product or service.

Vital 100 Wellness can serve as a new set of eyes to evaluate how your organization, company, or team is evolving and how to improve the bottom line and corporate culture.

Customization for Improving Performance

As we mentioned before, evaluating and developing a working plan will be customized for every organization, company or team we work with. Initiating a wellness, communication and performance program begins with an interview to determine the needs and goals of a group or team to then fully customize their program. This allows for the development of trust and clarity for our programs. The CEOs and directors undertaking our program comment on its effectiveness and the outcomes directed toward their goals. All CEOs, team owners, and organization directors are looking for ways to improve their organizations, companies and teams. The usual focus is to hire different people (based on reviews) or replace underperformers, beef up marketing, or add new products and services. These are all critical areas to improve performance and the bottom line, yet these areas are the focus of all companies, organizations, and teams.

Unfortunately, few groups utilize three other areas of focus, which are easy to incorporate, much less expensive and yield equally effective results regarding performance and, ultimately, the bottom line. These three little-understood areas to advance the bottom line are:

- Optimize health and wellness for everyone in a group (company, organization, team).
- Enhance communication skills within and outside your group.
- Develop a performance mentality.

Enhancing these three areas not only directly impacts your bottom line but also positively impacts sales and corporate culture while lowering overhead costs.

Tying It All Together

Can you imagine an entire group enthusiastically coming to work well rested and ready to give 100 percent for the entire day and not have 5 to 10 percent of your members or employees call in sick daily?

Think how wonderful it would be if every member of your company, organization or team was a marketer who believed in what your company produced as a direct result of your amazing corporate culture (enhanced wellness and communication skills), not just the responsibility of the marketing department. Highly performing companies looking for every advantage to take their company to higher levels agreed that a focus on health and wellness was imperative to their ongoing performance. Health, improved cognition, greater energy levels and developing a performance mindset with enhanced communication skills is the recipe for achieving any goal in your professional or personal life.

Vital 100 Wellness is the coaching company that can bring these areas of expertise to companies, groups and individuals with whom we work. Nevertheless, integrating each of these areas of expertise to customize your program is the true and unique expertise.

Good luck in your journey to an enhanced bottom line and corporate culture.

For more information, contact:
drbob@vital100wellness.com.

Thank You for Reading *Skyrocket Your Bottom Line!*

Your feedback matters to me. Please take a moment to head over to drbob@vital100wellness.com and share your thoughts in an honest review. Your reviews help others learn about the concepts in this book, and your honest feedback will make this and my future books better.

Thank You!

If you have more questions about our program, I am available for consultation. Join my subscriber list to stay connected, as well as for updates on my next book. I'd love to hear from you or work with you as you further improve your bottom line.

Let's Connect

Email: drbob@vital100wellness.com
Website: vital100wellness.com

By the way, if you haven't claimed your complimentary health consult, don't forget to do so today. I look forward to hearing about your progress.

Best in health and performance,

Dr. Bob Johnson

Acknowledgements

A consultant, expert or writer is not sought out by large groups of people without the mentoring and guidance by honest, influential people.

To this day, the greatest influencers in my life are my parents. My dad, Samuel, provided me with ethics, ongoing motivation, passion and an amazing role model, while my mother (Elizabeth, aka Bette) was always a loving, positive role model who showed me how to "walk in other's shoes."

My ongoing motivation comes from my sons Andrew and Nicolas, who provide me with reasons to continue to serve as a steady, loving, honest and successful role model. They have been instrumental in motivating me to write *Skyrocketing Your Bottom Line.*

I would be remiss not to acknowledge the myriad of mentors and teachers over several decades that have passed through my life and who urged me to be curious and to be comfortable challenging existing norms when those norms benefitted few or undermined the lives of a significant number of people and clients around me. Collectively, they have also provided me with the impetus to write this book.

I sincerely hope that I have served and continue to serve as an inspiration to others I have touched for many decades. Your successes and healthy journeys will always inspire me.

A special thanks to my siblings, Elizabeth, William and Susan, as well as Meena Samudre, who have shown me unconditional love, support, and honesty about what is truly important in life.

Hopefully, *Skyrocketing Your Bottom Line* will help to inspire others no matter their age and areas of focus.

For all, always remember to "enjoy the journey."

About the Author

Evolving along the journey into a top-level health coach and health consultant was littered with many ups and downs but truly exemplified the type of person Dr. Bob Johnson is. He was always interested in overall health, given his extensive athletic background and professional training in college and professional school. Simultaneously, he became a national class runner during his time in dental school.

Although becoming a dentist was very technical, Dr. Bob always enjoyed the health connection to dentistry. For 25 years, he honed his dental skills and became the dentist many people would travel from around the country to see because of his unique orientation to biologic dentistry. Nevertheless, his interests, skills, and training slowly pulled him away from cutting-edge chairside dentistry to work with the health and performance of individuals and eventually with organizations and teams.

Dr. Bob realized that he should follow his instincts to develop his true love of health coaching. He studied with not only the top practitioners in the world, but voraciously studied and applied his knowledge from many fields of health, combined with a love of people. This allowed him to quickly develop his abilities in the area of natural and integrative health.

As his results with many clients continued to evolve, he looked to leverage those skills with larger groups of people who could apply his work and knowledge to optimize their performance in business, athletics, and their personal life.

He developed the program of corporate wellness (www.Vital100Wellness.com), which combines unique, high-level health and lifestyle skills with communication skills enhancement, and performance (mindset) training. All three of these integrate and profoundly impact the advancement of the most important possession we all have: health. This is especially important in the world of business, which has pervasive, health compromising stress.

The greatest impediment to optimal health and high-level performance is misinformation or the lack of information. Dr. Bob's background (professional training and athletics) combined with the desire to provide what people truly need has been the motivation and energy to fuel the growth of this high-quality program of corporate wellness.

When great need meets highly passionate, highly skilled, and motivated people, great synergy evolves. The companies, organizations and teams Dr. Bob's wellness team work with experience a huge boost to their bottom line and the development of an exceptional, healthy corporate culture.

Contact drbob@vital100wellness.com to understand how this comprehensive, customized program can optimize your company's, organization's or team's performance.

Made in the USA
Columbia, SC
07 July 2023

19982182R00078